the Australian worship collection

BOOK TWO

First published in Great Britain in 2000 by world wide worship ltd.

© Copyright 2000 world wide worship ltd.

ISBN 1 84003 475 0
ISMN M 57004 629 4
Catalogue No: 1450162

0 1 2 3 4 5 6 7 8 9

Cover design by Jonathan Stroulger

Compiled by Asher Gregory
Music Setter: Donald Thomson
Proof-readers: Rob Danter and Helen Goodall

Important Copyright Information

The Publishers wish to express their gratitude to the copyright owners who have granted permission to include their copyright material in this book. Full details are indicated on the respective pages.

The **words** of most of the songs in this publication are covered by a **Church Copyright Licence** which allows local church reproduction on overhead projector acetates, in service bulletins, songsheets, audio/visual recording and other formats.

The **music** in this book is covered by the **Music Reproduction Licence** issued by CCL (Europe) Ltd (or CCLI in your respective territory) and you may photocopy the music and words of the songs in the book provided:

> You hold a current Music Reproduction Licence from CCL (Europe) Ltd.

> The copyright owner of the hymn or song you intend to photocopy is included in the Authorised Catalogue List which comes with your Music Reproduction Licence.

Full details of both the Church Copyright Licence and the additional Music Reproduction Licence are available from:

Christian Copyright Licensing (Europe) Ltd (or CCLI in your respective territory), PO Box 1339, Eastbourne, East Sussex BN21 1AD.
Tel: +44 (0)1323 417711; Fax: +44 (0)1323 417722; E-mail: info@ccli.com; Web: www.ccli.com.

Please note, all texts and music in this book are protected by copyright and if you do not possess a licence from CCL (Europe) Ltd (or CCLI in your respective territory), they may not be reproduced in any way for sale or private use without the consent of the copyright owner.

the Australian worship collection

Spanning the first ten years of praise and worship music from Hillsong Music Australia and Geoff Bullock

FULL MUSIC 1450104

Accompanying the Full Music edition are two books containing arrangements for C and B♭ instruments

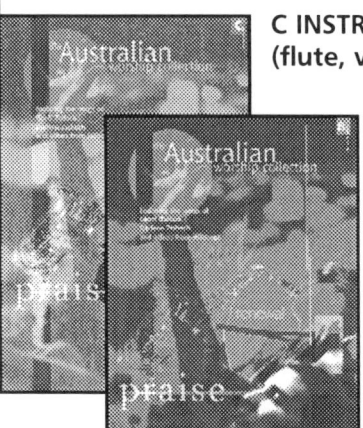

C INSTRUMENTS 1400189
(flute, violin, recorder and oboe)

B♭ INSTRUMENTS 1400188
(clarinet, trumpet and tenor sax)

www • Buxhall • Stowmarket • IP14 3BW
Tel:+44(0)1449 737978 Fax:+44(0)1449 737834
E-mail: info@kevinmayhewltd.com

Foreword

We are honoured to have our songs included in this collection of Australian worship music. Our mandate and mission is to declare the name of our awesome Lord through praise and worship in spirit and in truth, to all the ends of the earth . . .

Join us as we unite our voice, connect our hearts, shout his praise, and see the glory of his presence fall on every nation, tribe and tongue.

Live to worship God.

DARLENE ZSCHECH - Worship Pastor - Hillsong Music Australia.

I am thrilled that Asher Gregory and Kevin Mayhew Publishers have put together this collection of favourite Australian praise and worship songs.

A fresh sound of worship is sweeping the earth and it is coming from every corner. It is the sound of freedom, great joy and of hearts which are grateful to God.

When we worship the Lord, we proclaim the reality of his endless kingdom. My prayer is that you will be blessed, and the world will be transformed as you bring God wonderful praise and worship.

RUSSELL FRAGAR - Music Director - Hillsong Music Australia.

I believe that God's hand is on Australian praise and worship; it's relevant – it touches today's society; it's generic – it reaches across all cultures; it's evangelistic – it bridges the gap; it's expressive – it unlocks the heart of man to touch the heart of God. What a privilege it is for me to be a part of *The Australian Worship Collection 2*.

MICHAEL DALTON

Geographically Australia is a rough and raw country. Our Australian style of music can be described as close to the heart, burning with passion and full of raw energy. Australian praise and worship is accepted around the globe because of its freshness and creative approach to contemporary church worship.

Australia was founded with a pioneering spirit only 200 years ago, and the pioneering spirit is obviously present in the heart of each songwriter and worship leader today.

I consider it a privilege to write songs to the glory of God, and am blessed in having them used for church worship across the world. Thanks for including us in the second edition of *The Australian Worship Collection*.

ANDREW IRONSIDE - Arrowhead Ministries.

A new sound is emerging in Australia that is literally touching the planet. God loves to birth his vision and purpose in places that the world would least expect: places that may not appear to be globally significant.

It's exciting to see God use worship music from 'down under' to inspire and impact so many churches from other nations and I feel privileged to be part of this Australian collection. I pray that the songs in this music book will greatly encourage your heart.

COLIN BATTERSBY - Music Director Lakes Christian Life Centre.

There is no doubt that over the past decade God has been doing something powerful in this part of the world in terms of praise and worship. Songwriters are rising up from all throughout Australia and New Zealand taking this 'new' sound of worship to the Body of Christ at large. The exciting thing is that many of these songs are now being sung, and having significant impact all over the globe.

We are thrilled to be included in this second edition of *The Australian Worship Collection*. May God touch you greatly as you listen to this Holy Spirit-inspired compilation.

PAUL ZAIA - Music Director - Sounds of Paradise.

Australia is an incredibly young nation. Young things grow quickly and the sound that is emerging from Auzzie churches is rapidly capturing the attention of worshippers all over the world. It's fresh, it's raw, it has a transparent innocence about it that allows people to connect with God in a myriad of ways from intimate worship ballads to vibrant and fiery praise choruses.

Our most anointed time of worship and service to the Lord is *now*. Faith is *now* – the day of salvation is *now* – the harvest is white *now*. Let's get into the presence of God *now*. Let's enjoy these offerings from 'down under'.

MICHAEL BATTERSBY - Assistant Pastor and Music Director - Christian Outreach Centre, Perth.

Praise and worship is the heart's response to the grace and mercy of God revealed to us in Jesus. This grace, so unmerited, so free, overwhelms hopelessness, humiliates guilt and compels us to rise out of the consequences of our failures. Mercy challenges us to live as though we are indebted to a pardon that we couldn't possibly earn or deserve.

The more I look at this grace and mercy, the more I am challenged to live graciously and mercifully. As I approach my piano, I have to remind myself that the songs are just a poor reflection of a greater truth that must be lived before it is sung. Jesus inspires me to live worshipfully. This 'life', this 'attitude' inspires me to sing, but my 'worship' and my 'praise' must remain the outworking of life and relationships before it ever becomes songs and services.

This volume of songs contains lyrics and melodies that can challenge us to sing, or inspire us to live. I pray that, as you 'look through' the windows of these lyrics you will see a greater truth: Jesus, his grace, his mercy, God revealed to us. In 'seeing him' through the songs, let all of us rise to live 'worshipfully'. Only then can these songs be called 'worship', for only then will our words be a reflection of the life that he has come to give.

Jesus is the word made flesh. Let these songs come to life in you. Then all the world will sing!

GEOFF BULLOCK

1 A heart of love

Heart of love

Words and Music: Geoff Bullock

© Copyright 1997 Watershed Productions. Administered by Kingsway's Thankyou Music, P.O. Box 75, Eastbourne, East Sussex BN23 6NW, UK. Used by permission.

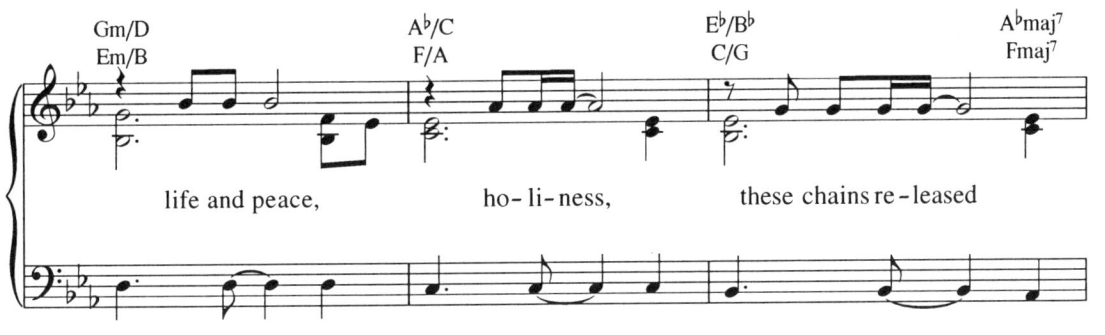
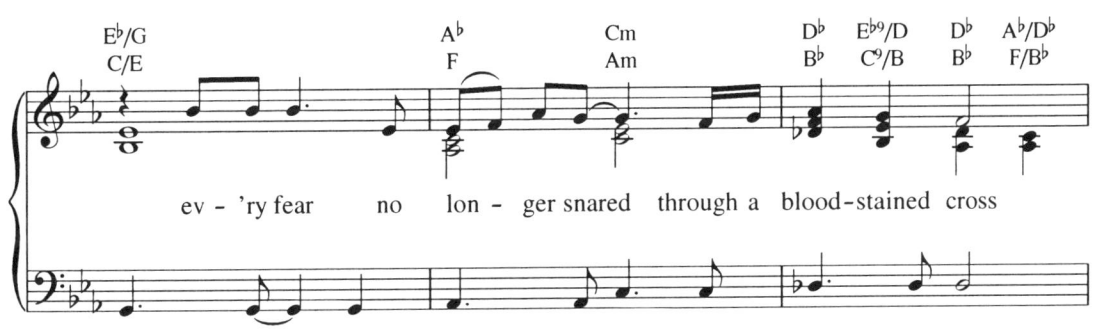

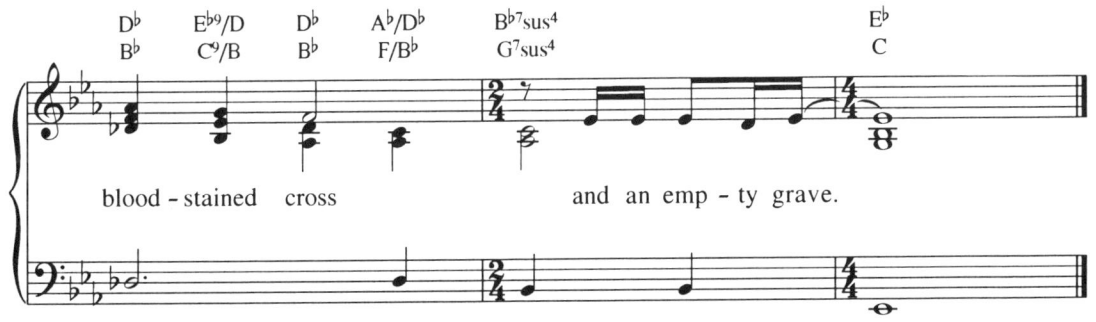

2 Ah Jesus, Jesus
Your name is so beautiful

Words and Music: Andrew Ironside

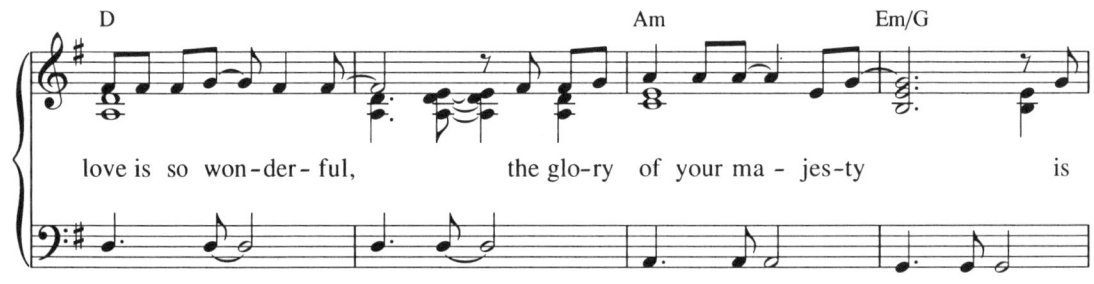

© Copyright 1997 Ironspiration Music, P.O. Box 226, Woombye,
Queensland 4559, Australia. Used by permission.

3 All creation bows
The word is out
Words and Music: Mick Dalton

© Copyright 2000 Kevin Mayhew Ltd.

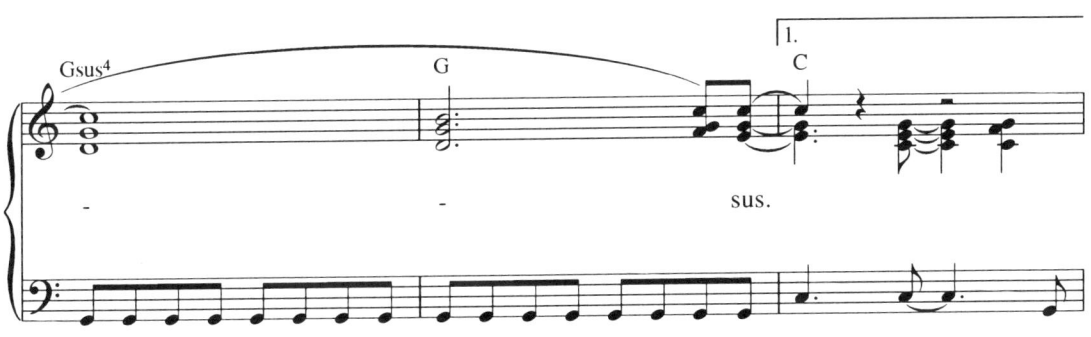

4 All honour, all glory

Words and Music: Chris Falson

© Copyright Chris Falson Music/Maranatha! Music. Administered by CopyCare,
P.O. Box 77, Hailsham, East Sussex BN27 3EF, UK (music@copycare.com). Used by permission.

5 All I know

Words and Music: Ian and Lucy Fisher

© Copyright 1998 Lucy and Ian Fisher/Hillsongs Publishing. Administered by Kingsway's Thankyou Music,
P.O. Box 75, Eastbourne, East Sussex BN23 6NW, UK. Used by permission.

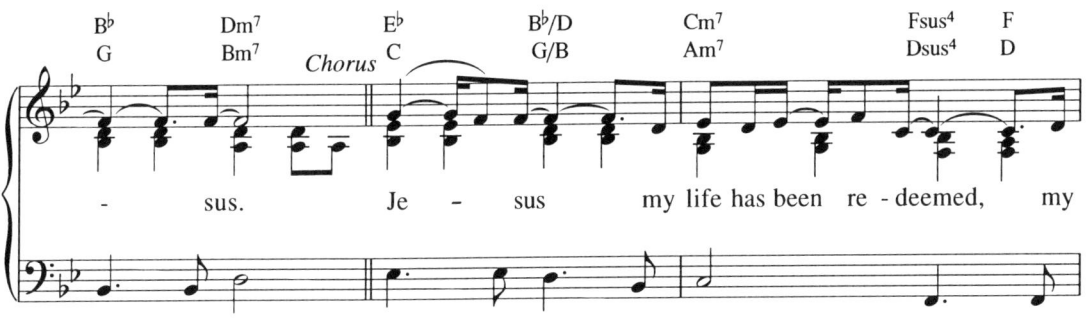

6 All that is within me, Lord
Sing of your great love

Words and Music: Darlene Zschech

© Copyright 1999 Darlene Zschech/Hillsongs Publishing. Administered by Kingsway's Thankyou Music, P.O. Box 75, Eastbourne, East Sussex BN23 6NW, UK. Used by permission.

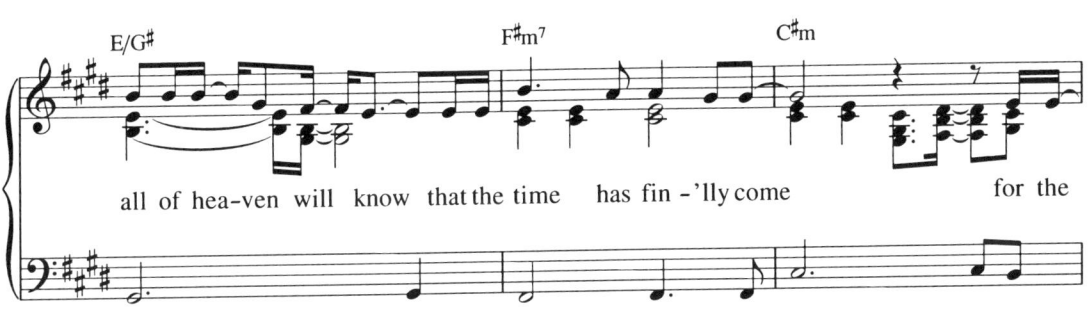

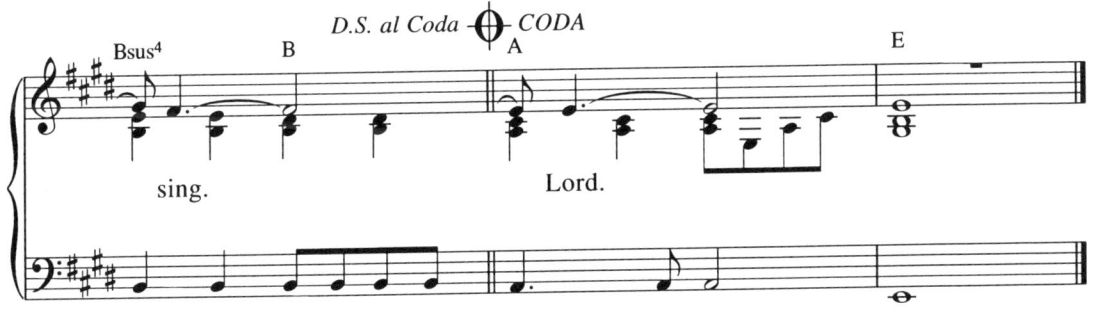

7 Anoint my hands for battle

Words and Music: Condy Canuto

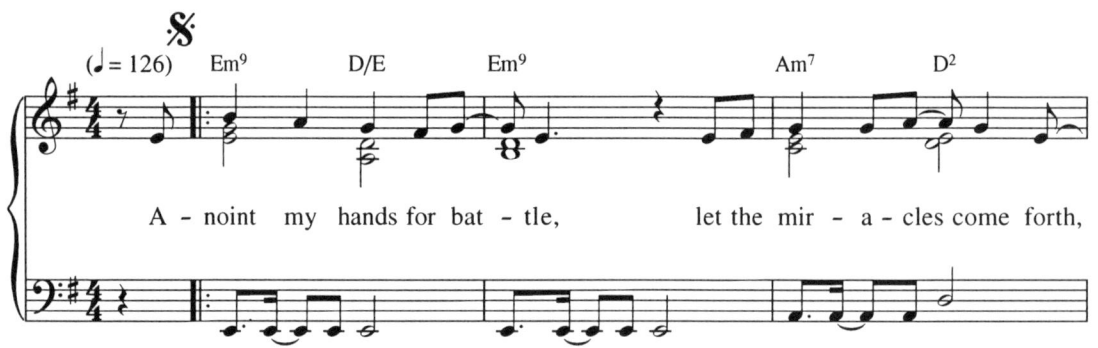

© Copyright 1997 Ironspiration Music, P.O. Box 228, Woombye,
Queensland 4559, Australia. Used by permission.

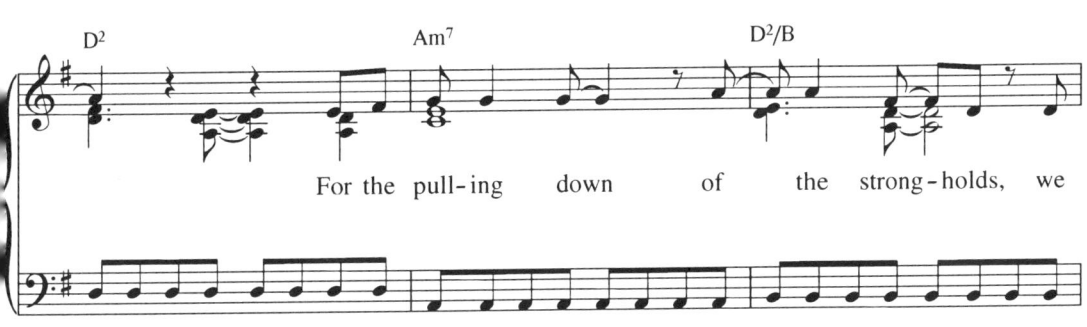
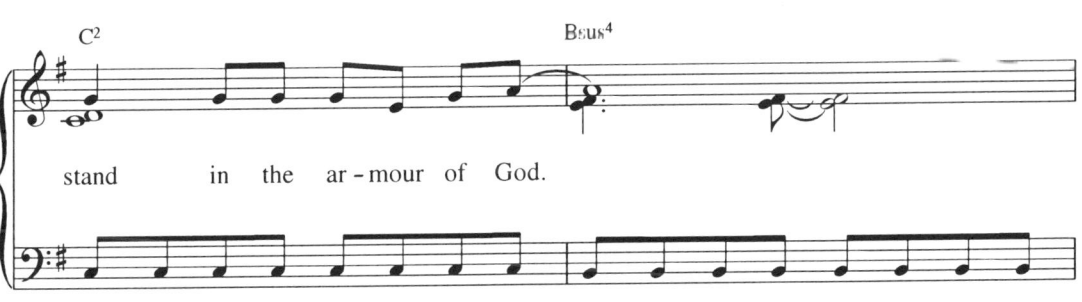

8 A rising generation
In freedom

Words and Music: Arun Puddle

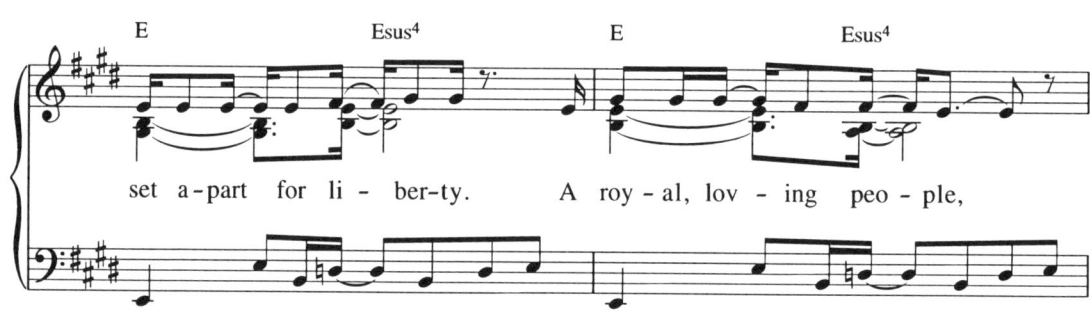
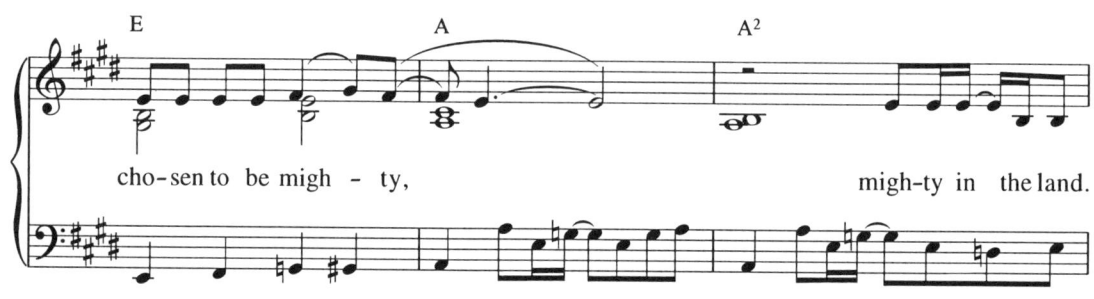

© Copyright 1998 Arun Puddle/Hillsongs Publishing. Administered by Kingsway's Thankyou Music, P.O. Box 75, Eastbourne, East Sussex BN23 6NW, UK. Used by permission.

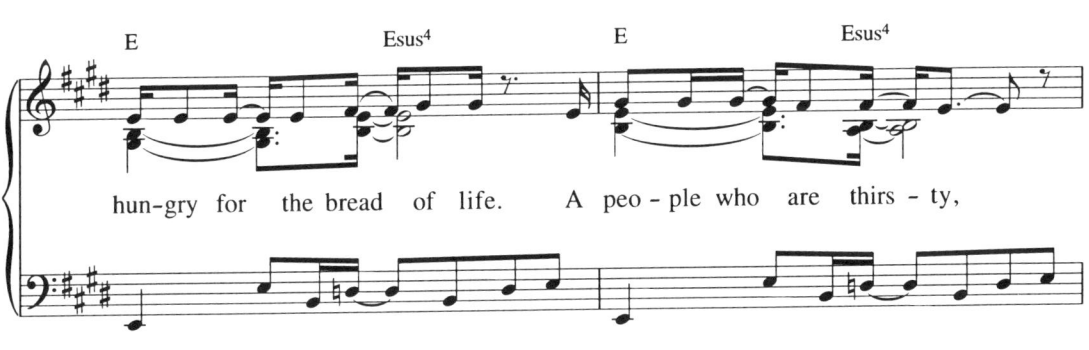
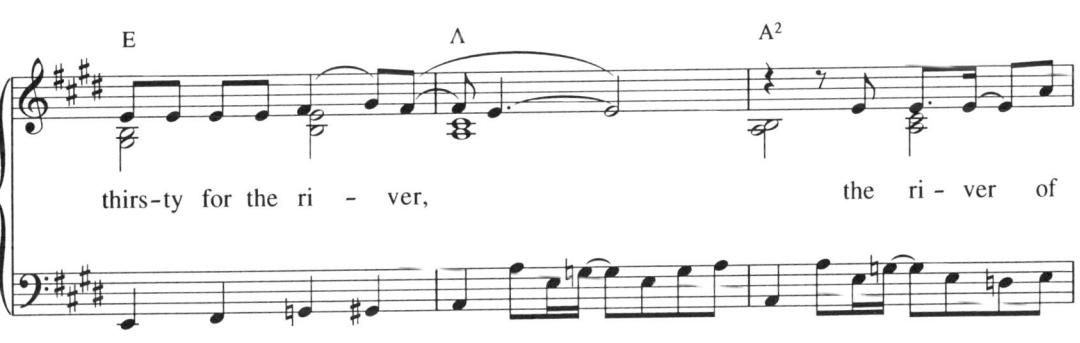

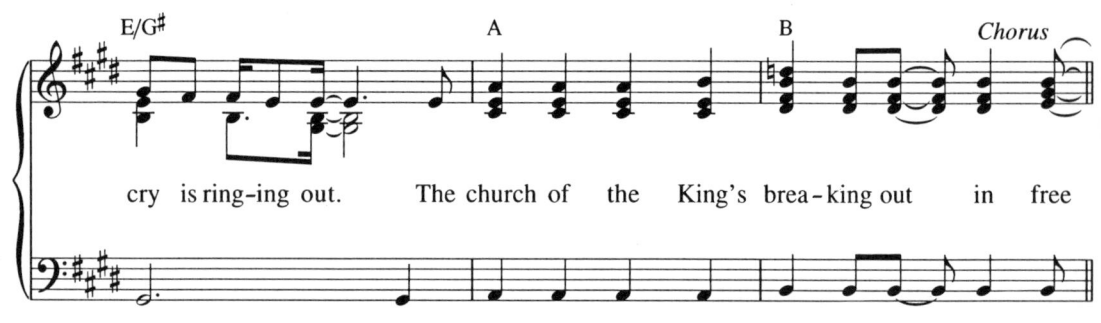

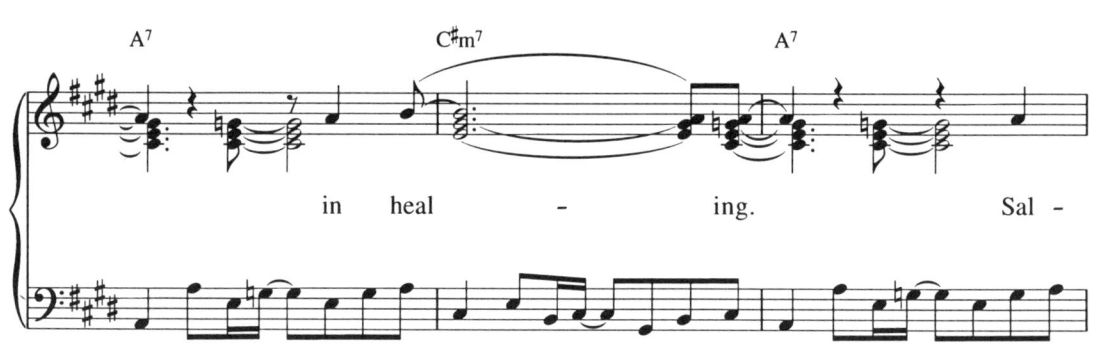
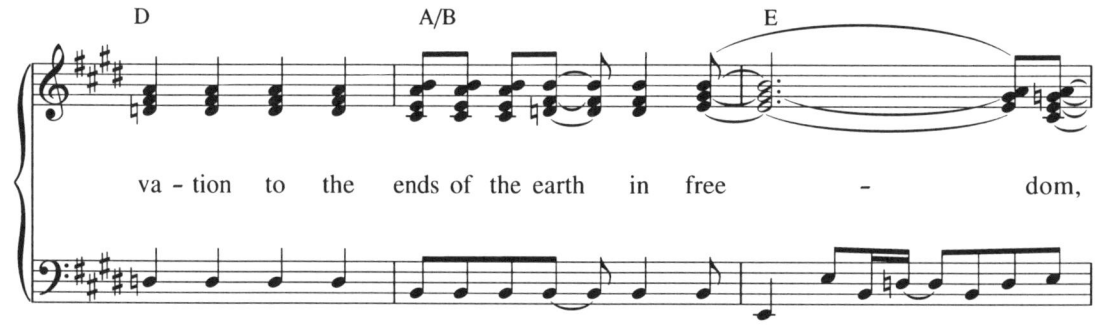

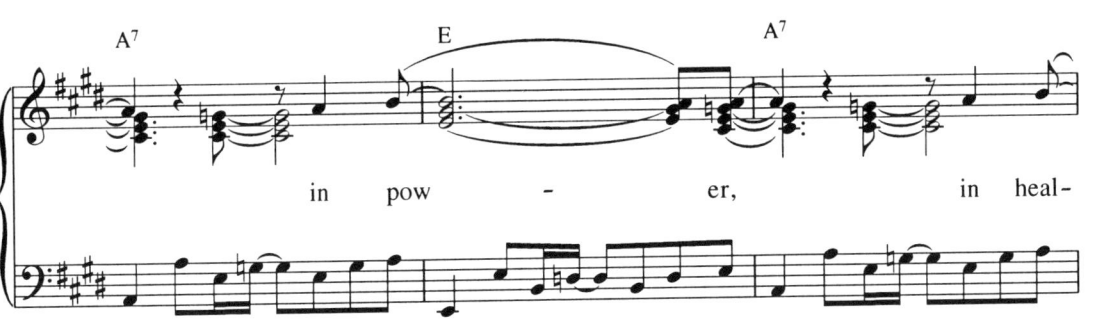

9 As I come to you

One in spirit

Words and Music: Mick Dalton

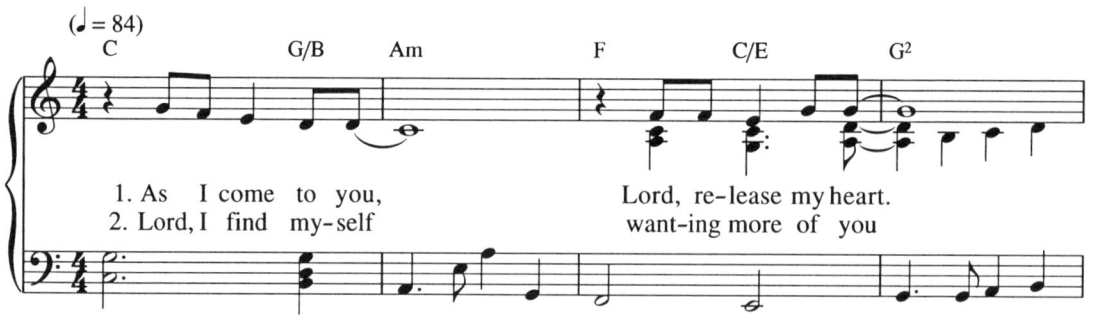
1. As I come to you, Lord, re-lease my heart.
2. Lord, I find my-self want-ing more of you

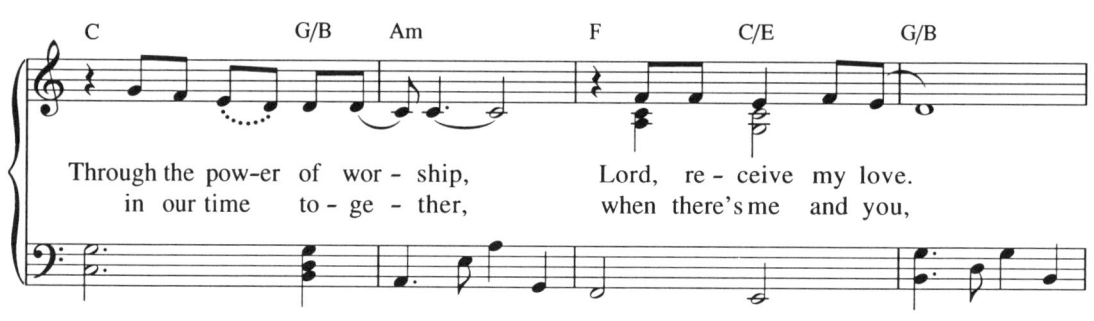
Through the pow-er of wor - ship, Lord, re - ceive my love.
in our time to - ge - ther, when there's me and you,

In this time of grace, let your pre - sence fall.
I can lay be - fore you all my heart can't hold.

We're at one in Spi - rit, in this time of ours.

© Copyright 1999 Kevin Mayhew Ltd.

10 As we lift our hands to worship you

So let us rise to worship

Words and Music: Geoff Bullock

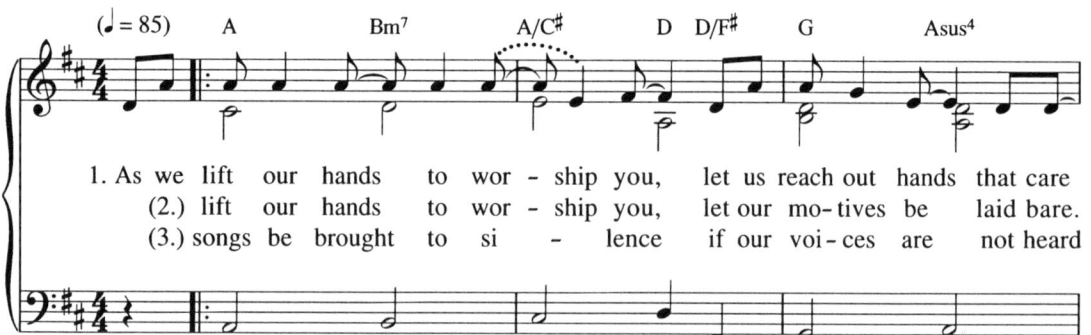

1. As we lift our hands to wor-ship you, let us reach out hands that care
(2.) lift our hands to wor-ship you, let our mo-tives be laid bare.
(3.) songs be brought to si - lence if our voi-ces are not heard

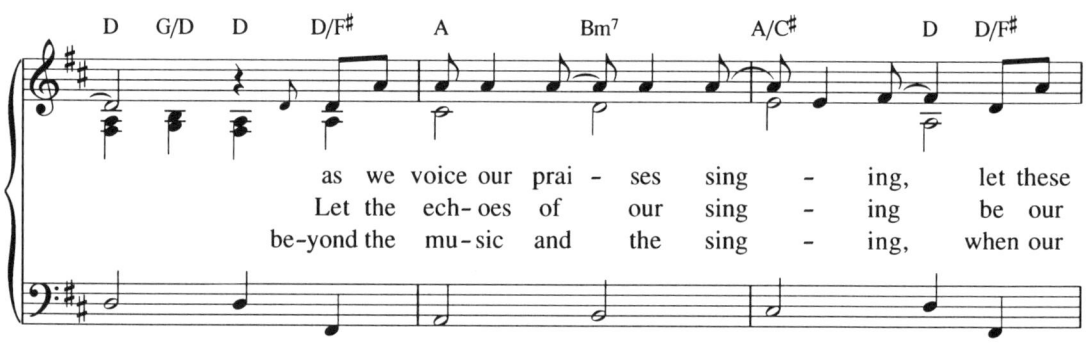

as we voice our prai-ses sing - ing, let these
Let the ech-oes of our sing - ing be our
be-yond the mu-sic and the sing - ing, when our

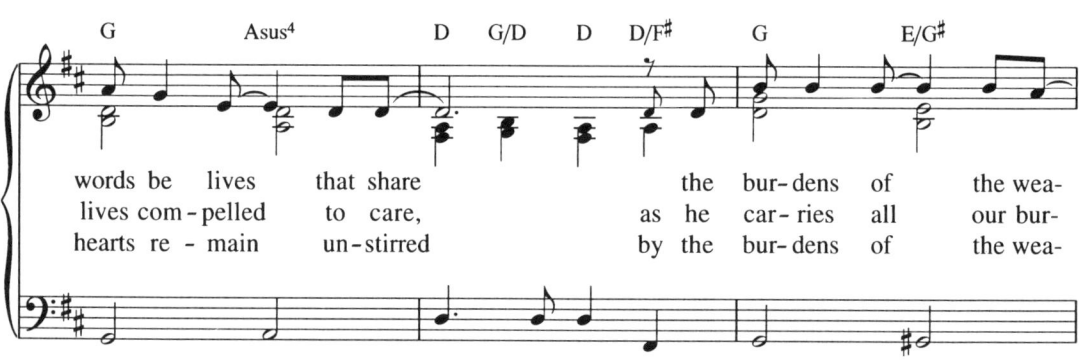

words be lives that share the bur-dens of the wea-
lives com-pelled to care, as he car-ries all our bur-
hearts re-main un-stirred by the bur-dens of the wea-

© Copyright 1999 Watershed Productions. Administered by Kingsway's Thankyou Music,
P.O. Box 75, Eastbourne, East Sussex BN23 6NW, UK. Used by permission.

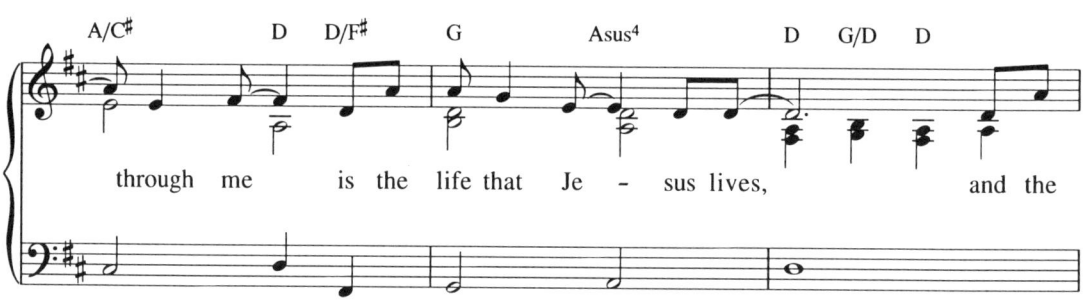
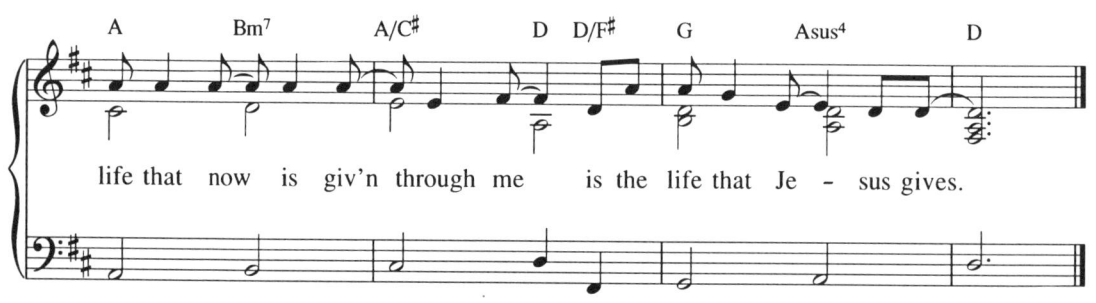

11 Beautiful Lord, wonderful Saviour

The Potter's hand

Words and Music: Darlene Zschech

© Copyright 1997 Darlene Zschech/Hillsongs Publishing/Kingsway's Thankyou Music,
P.O. Box 75, Eastbourne, East Sussex BN23 6NW, UK. Used by permission.

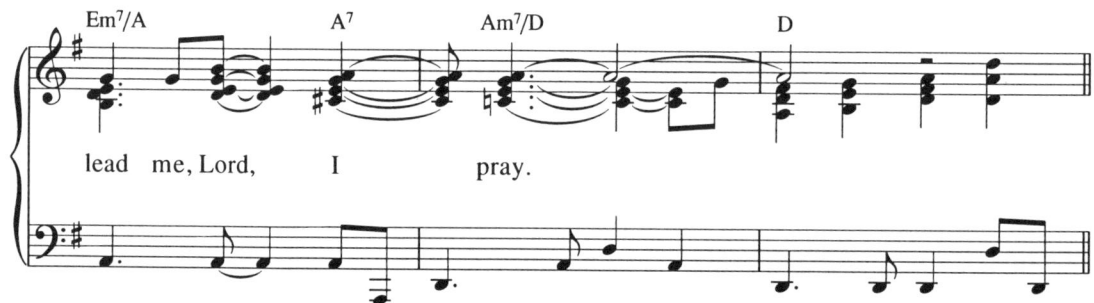

12 Beautiful Saviour

Words and Music: Geoff Bullock

© Copyright 1999 Watershed Productions. Administered by Kingsway's Thankyou Music,
P.O. Box 75, Eastbourne, East Sussex BN23 6NW, UK. For the UK only. Used by permission.

13 Breathe on me

Words and Music: Lucy Fisher

1. Breathe on me, breath of God, love and life that makes me free. Breathe on me, breath of God, fan the flame within me.
2. Speak to me, voice of God, soft and still inside my heart. Speak to me, word of God, comfort, heal restore with love.

Chorus
Teach my heart, heal my soul, speak the mind that in

© Copyright 1999 Lucy Fisher/Hillsongs Publishing. Administered by Kingsway's Thankyou Music, P.O. Box 75, Eastbourne, East Sussex BN23 6NW, UK. Used by permission.

14 Come, let's lift our praise
Lift our praise

Words and Music: Geoff Bullock

© Copyright 1999 Watershed Productions. Administered by Kingsway's Thankyou Music, P.O. Box 75, Eastbourne, East Sussex BN23 6NW, UK. For the UK only. Used by permission.

15 Creation stands in awe

Words and Music: Geoff Bullock

Cre-a-tion stands in awe of you, all cre-a-tion formed and filled by you: ev-'ry pla-net, ev-'ry star in the hea-vens near or far, all that e-ver was or e-ver is to be. All cre-a-tion by your hand, all ac-cord-ing to your per-fect plan;

mer-cy's pure and per-fect plan giv-ing all for fal-len man a sac-ri-fice of o-ver-whelm-ing grace and love. Our re-demp-tion by your hand, all ac-cord-ing to your per-fect plan;

© Copyright 1999 Watershed Productions. Administered by Kingsway's Thankyou Music, P.O. Box 75, Eastbourne, East Sussex BN23 6NW, UK. For the UK only. Used by permission.

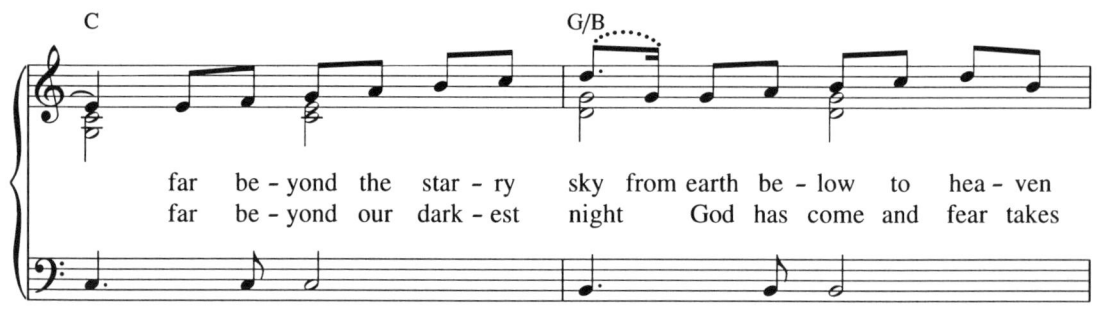

16 Deeper and deeper

Words and Music: Geoff Bullock

© Copyright 1999 Watershed Productions. Administered by Kingsway's Thankyou Music,
P.O. Box 75, Eastbourne, East Sussex BN23 6NW, UK. For the UK only. Used by permission.

17 Forever loved by you
Forever and always

Words and Music: Geoff Bullock

Forever loved by you, Lord I am forever loved by you.

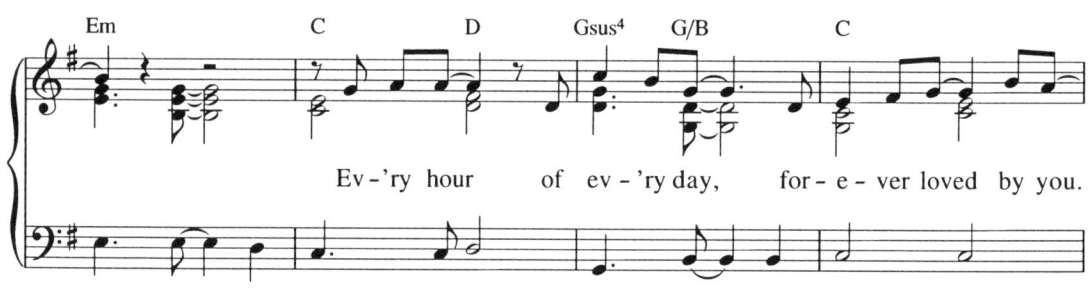
Ev'ry hour of ev'ry day, forever loved by you.

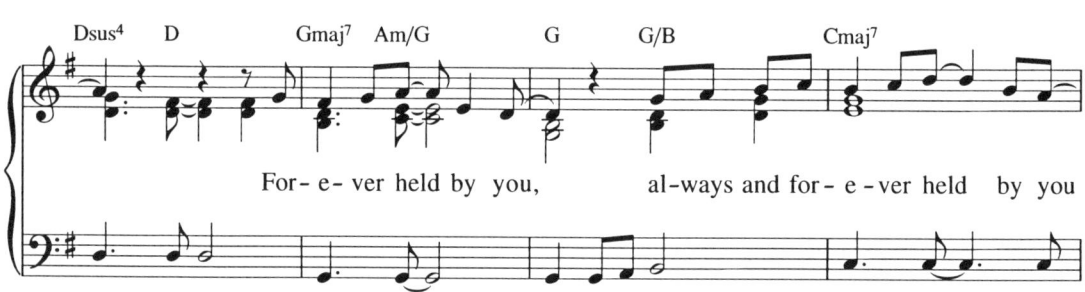
Forever held by you, always and forever held by you

through ev'ry storm and ev'ry night, forever loved by you.

© Copyright 1999 Watershed Productions. Administered by Kingsway's Thankyou Music, P.O. Box 75, Eastbourne, East Sussex BN23 6NW, UK. For the UK only. Used by permission.

18 Freedom and liberty

Words and Music: Michael Battersby

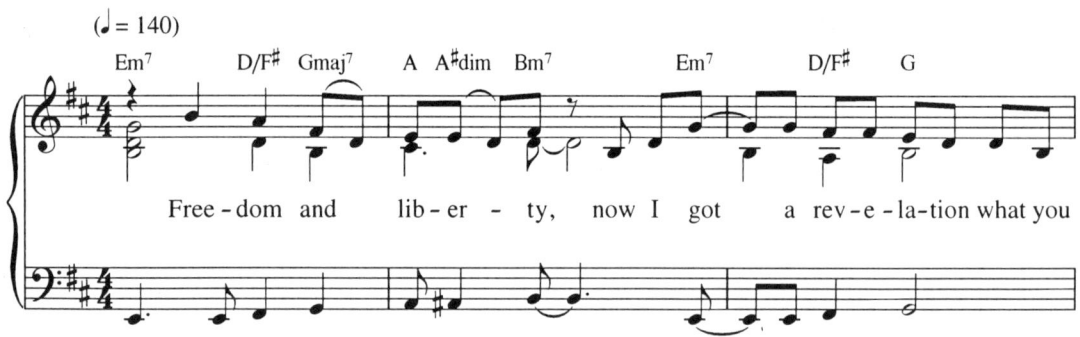

© Copyright 1996 Michael Battersby/Smart Productions, P.O. Box 82,
Victoria Park, WA 6100, Australia. Used by permission.

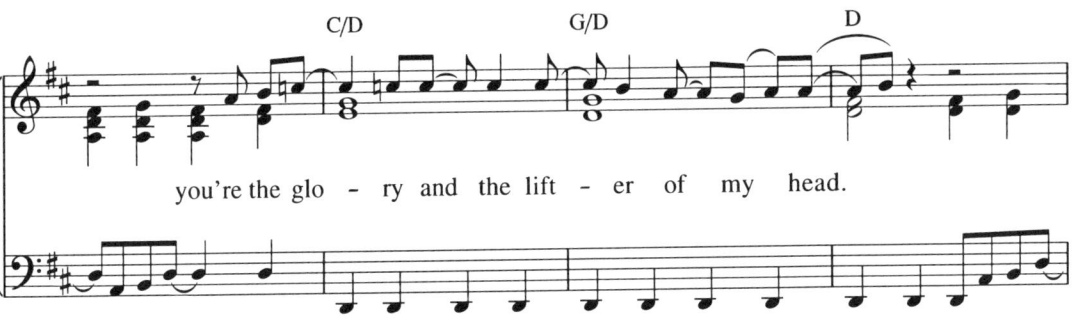

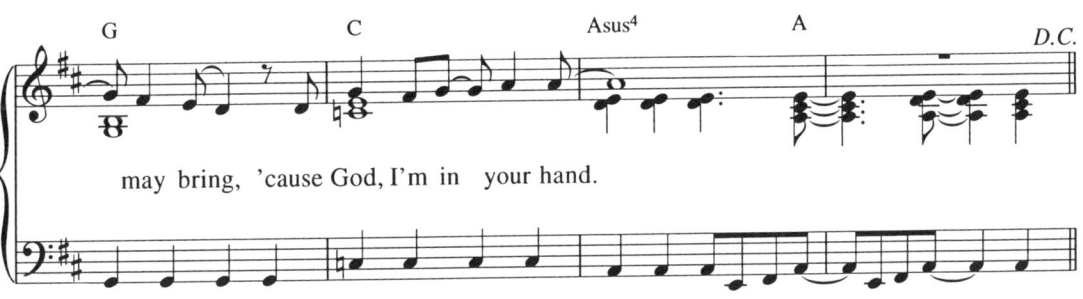

19 God Almighty, let your presence
Let your glory fall

Words and Music: Michael Battersby

© Copyright 1996 Michael Battersby/Smart Productions, P.O. Box 82, Victoria Park, WA 6100, Australia. Used by permission.

20 God says 'Yes'
Yes and Amen

Words and Music: Russell Fragar

© Copyright 1997 Russell Fragar/Hillsongs Publishing. Administered by Kingsway's Thankyou Music, P.O. Box 75, Eastbourne, East Sussex BN23 6NW, UK. Used by permission.

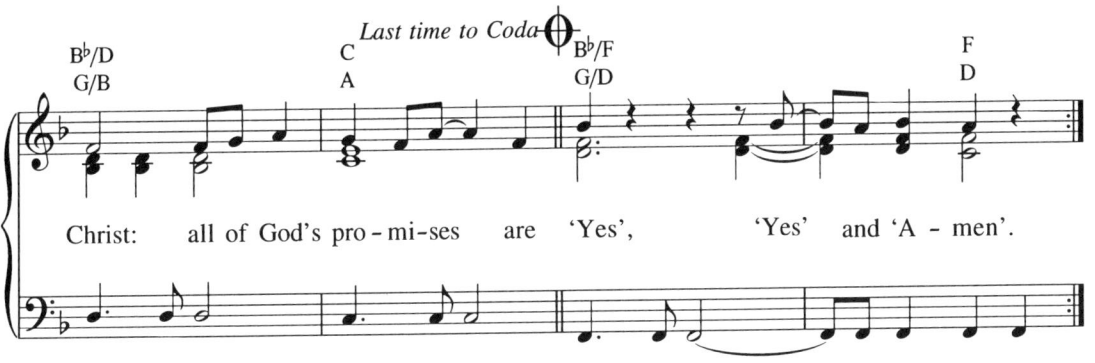

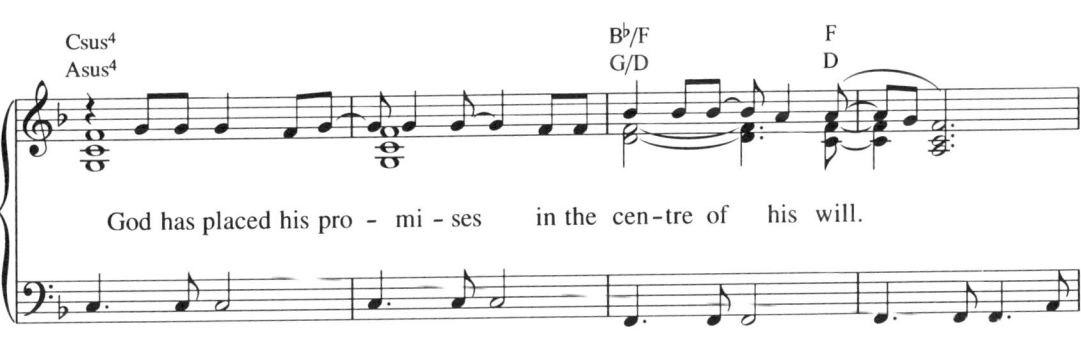

21 Heaven above and earth below
Grace abounds to all

Words and Music: Geoff Bullock

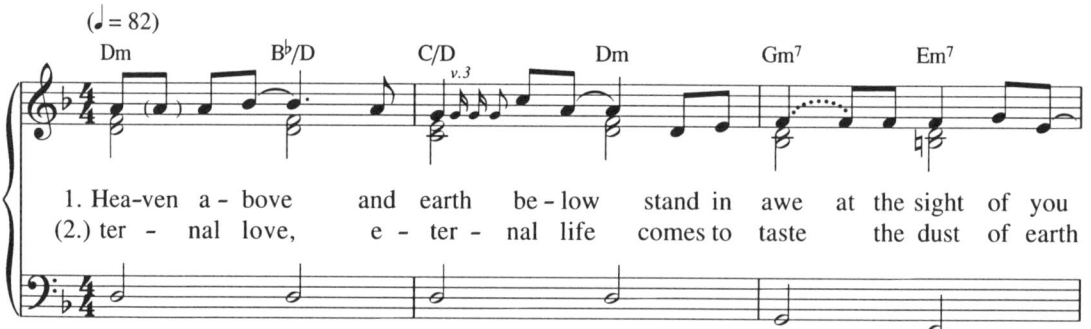
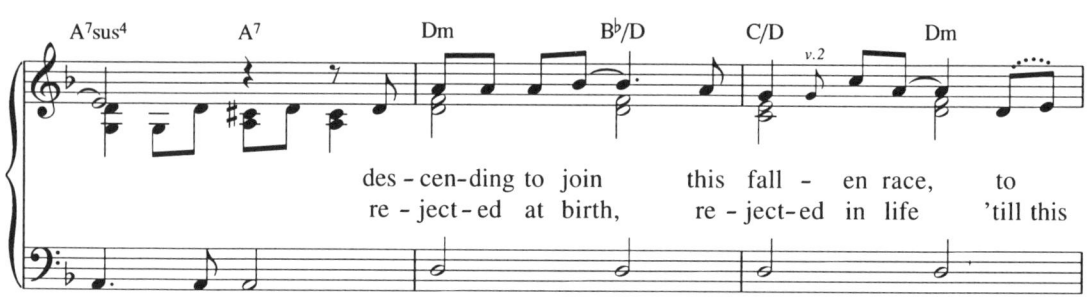
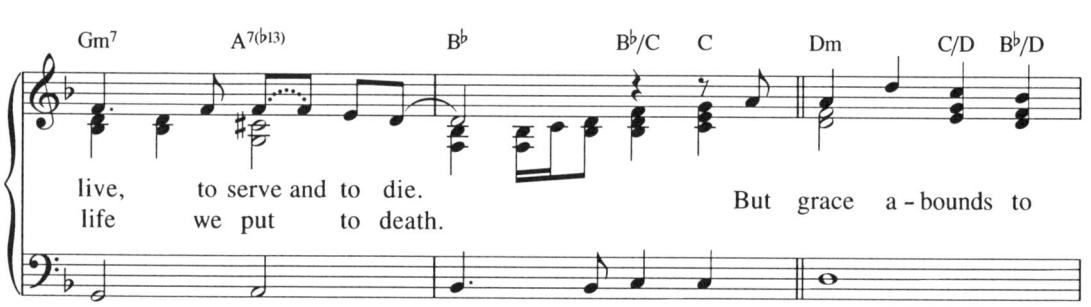
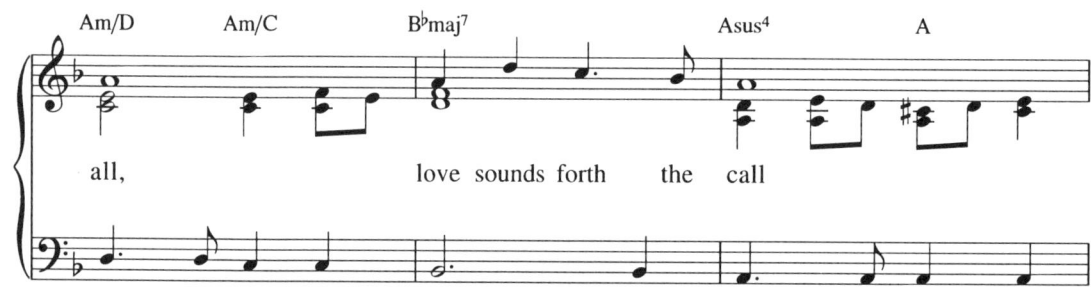

1. Heaven above and earth below stand in awe at the sight of you descending to join this fallen race, to live, to serve and to die. But grace abounds to all, love sounds forth the call

(2.) ternal love, eternal life comes to taste the dust of earth rejected at birth, rejected in life 'till this life we put to death.

© Copyright 1999 Watershed Productions. Administered by Kingsway's Thankyou Music, P.O. Box 75, Eastbourne, East Sussex BN23 6NW, UK. For the UK only. Used by permission.

life has come to take our place as his

death be-comes our life. 2. E - life.

3. Mercy has come unmerited and free
   while the guilt still stained our hands.
   Grace now leads us to the truth
   of the lives he came to save.

22 Here I am waiting
Eagles' wings

Words and Music: Darlene Zschech

Here I am wait-ing, a-bide in me I pray,

here I am long-ing for you.

Hide me in your love, bring me to my knees,

may I know Je-sus more and more.

© Copyright 1998 Reuben Morgan/Hillsongs Publishing. Administered by Kingsway's Thankyou Music, P.O. Box 75, Eastbourne, East Sussex BN23 6NW, UK. Used by permission.

23 Here in your presence

Words and Music: Colin Battersby

© Copyright 1998 Colin Battersby/Lakes Music Australia, P.O. Box 1038, Wangara, WA 6947, Australia. Used by permission.

25 Holy, holy, holy

Words and Music: Andrew and Desme Ironside

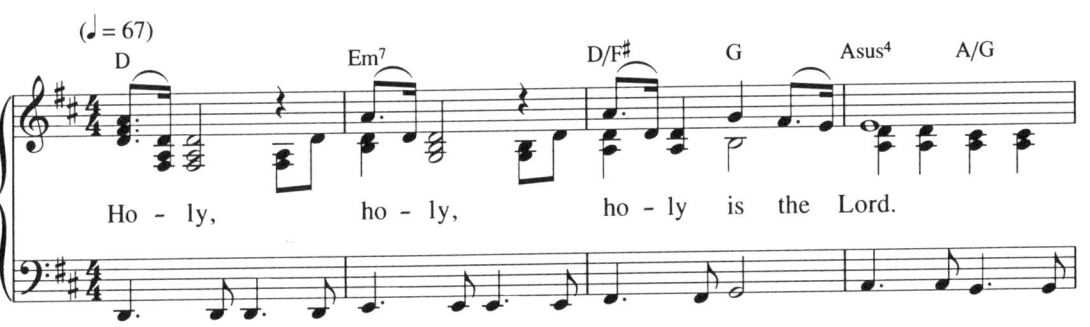

© Copyright 1997 Ironspiration Music, P.O. Box 228, Woombye, Queensland 4559, Australia. Used by permission.

26 Holy Spirit, I surrender
Child of grace

Words and Music: Mick Dalton

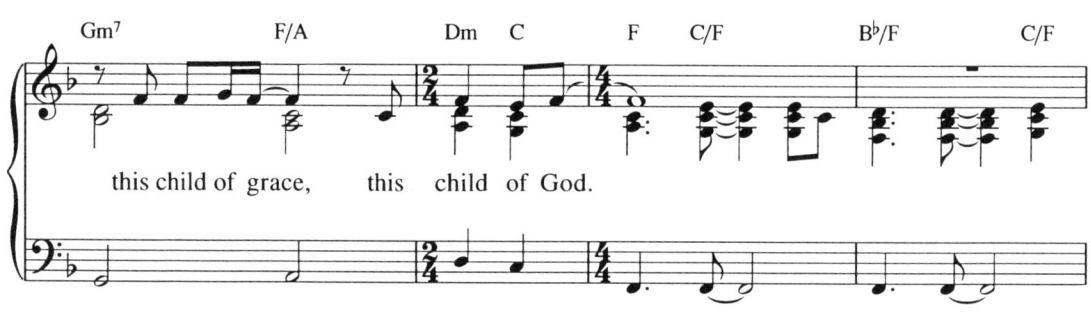

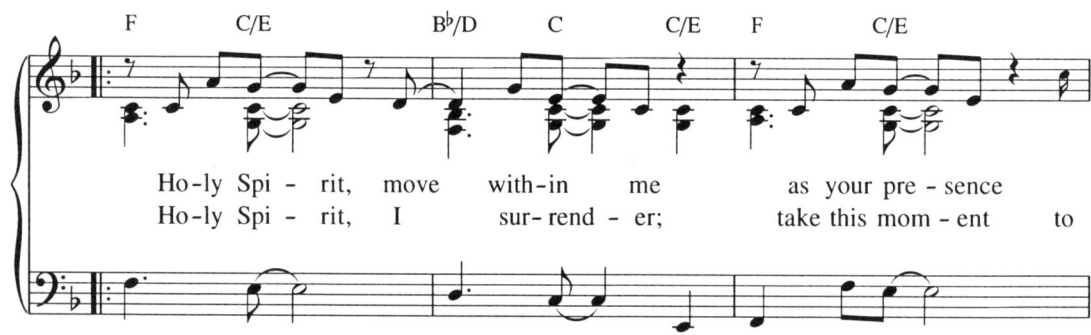

© Copyright 2000 Kevin Mayhew Ltd.

27 Holy Spirit, rain down

Words and Music: Russell Fragar

© Copyright 1997 Russell Fragar/Hillsongs Publishing/Kingsway's Thankyou Music, P.O. Box 75, Eastbourne, East Sussex BN23 6NW, UK. Used by permission.

28 I am not the same
Stay

Words and Music: Luke Munns

© Copyright 1999 Luke Munns/Hillsongs Publishing. Administered by Kingsway's Thankyou Music, P.O. Box 75, Eastbourne, East Sussex BN23 6NW, UK. Used by permission.

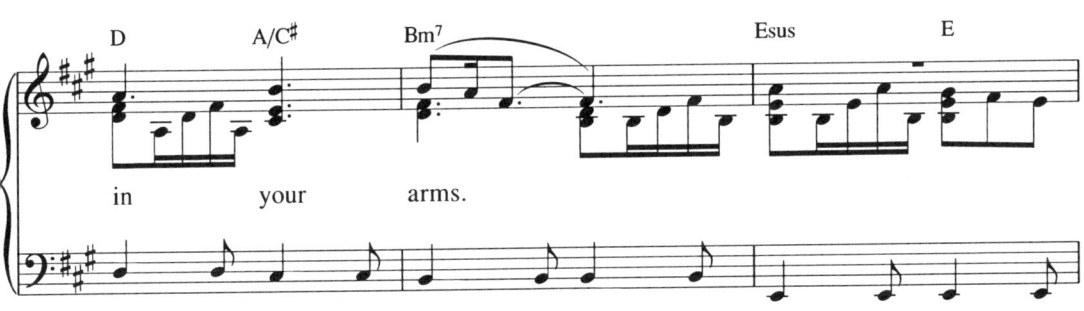

29 I believe

Words and Music: Colin Battersby

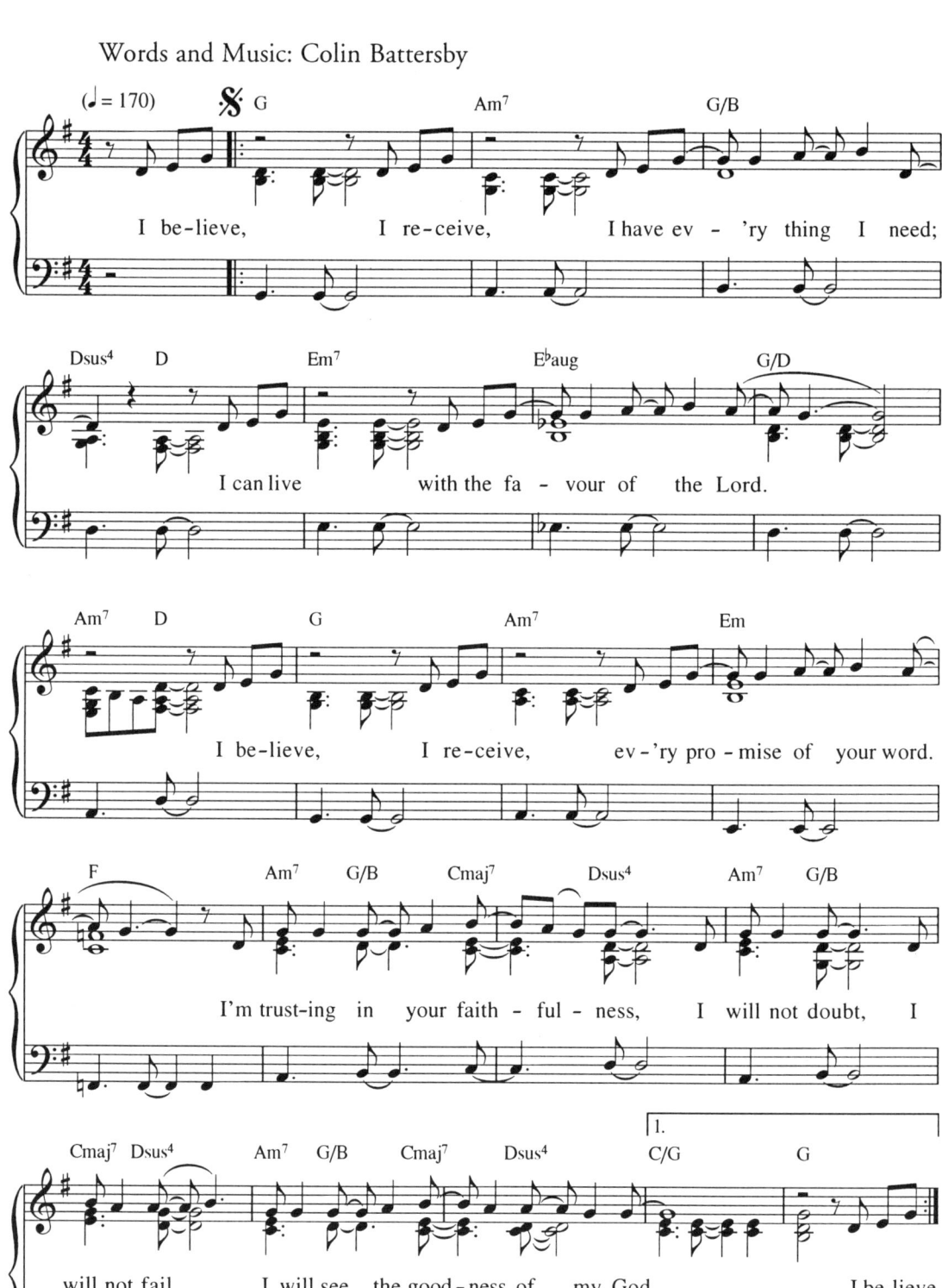

© Copyright 1999 Colin Battersby/Lakes Music Australia, P.O. Box 1038, Wangara, WA 6947, Australia. Used by permission.

30 I can feel

Words and Music: David Evans

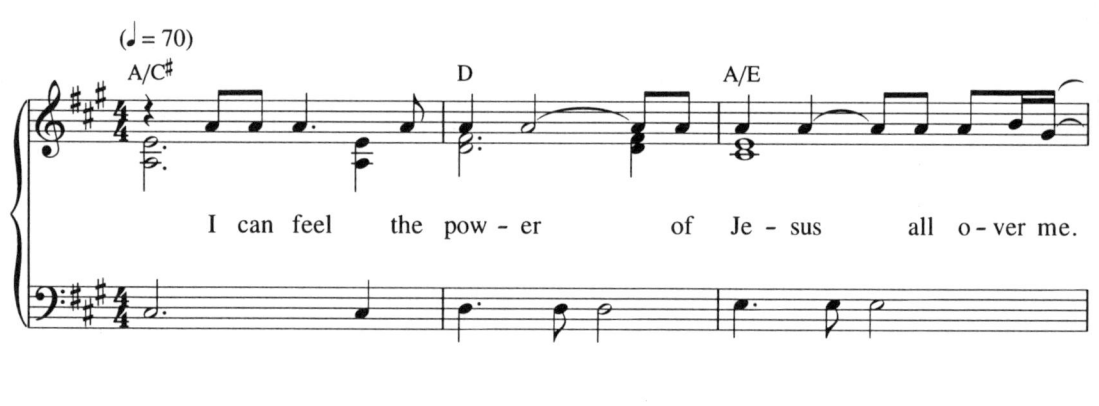

I can feel the pow-er of Je-sus all o-ver me.

Sounds like a rush-ing wind, a ho-ly

fi-re fills this place. Let me stand in awe and

wor-ship the God of sav-ing grace.

© Copyright 1994 Heartfelt Music, 84 Sherry Street,
Carseldine, QLD 4034, Australia. Used by permission.

31 I can feel the Spirit of God is moving

Pour on your power

Words and Music: Michael Battersby

© Copyright 1998 Michael Battersby/Smart Productions, P.O. Box 82,
Victoria Park, WA 6100, Australia. Used by permission.

32 I can hear heaven calling

Deeper

Words and Music: Colin Battersby

© Copyright 1999 Colin Battersby/Lakes Music Australia, P.O. Box 1038,
Wangara, WA 6947, Australia. Used by permission.

33 I can see the day
To the glory of your name

Words and Music: Reuben Morgan

1. I can see the day when walls of darkness fall,
And nations sound the praise my Redeemer lives.
Broken lives will be restored, rich and poor will be released.

2. I can see the day when children silence wars,
And on our knees we'll pray the greatest victory,
We will cry out for the lost, we will see the dying live.

© Copyright 1998 Reuben Morgan/Hillsongs Publishing. Administered by Kingsway's Thankyou Music, P.O. Box 75, Eastbourne, East Sussex BN23 6NW, UK. Used by permission.

34 I know he rescued my soul
My Redeemer lives

Words and Music: Reuben Morgan

© Copyright 1998 Reuben Morgan/Hillsongs Publishing/Kingsway's Thankyou Music,
P.O. Box 75, Eastbourne, East Sussex BN23 6NW, UK. Used by permission.

You lift my bur - den, I'll rise with you:

I'm danc-ing on this moun - tain top to

see your king - dom come. My Re -

35 I lift up my eyes to your throne
River

Words and Music: Darlene Zschech and Reuben Morgan

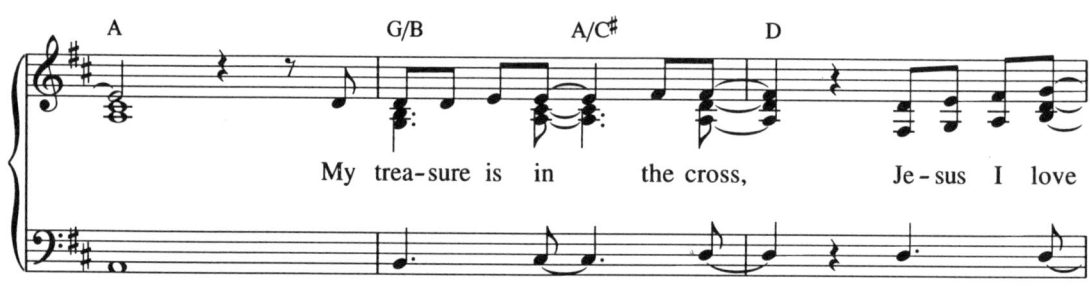

© Copyright 1998 Hillsongs Publishing/Kingsway's Thankyou Music, P.O. Box 75, Eastbourne, East Sussex BN23 6NW, UK. Used by permission.

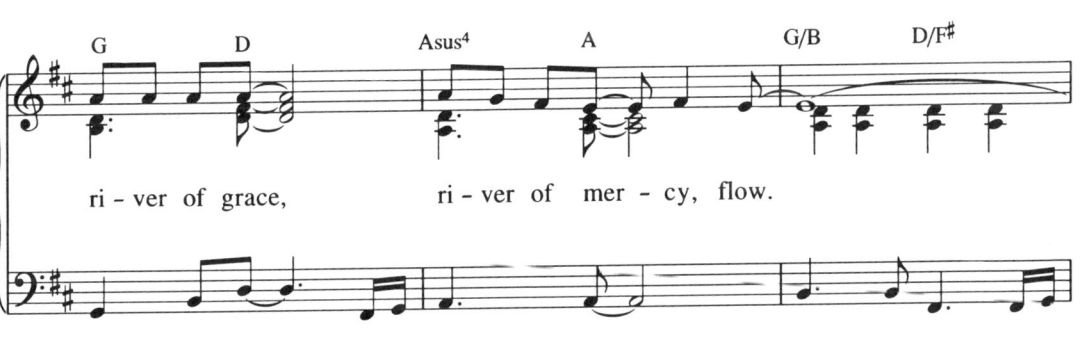

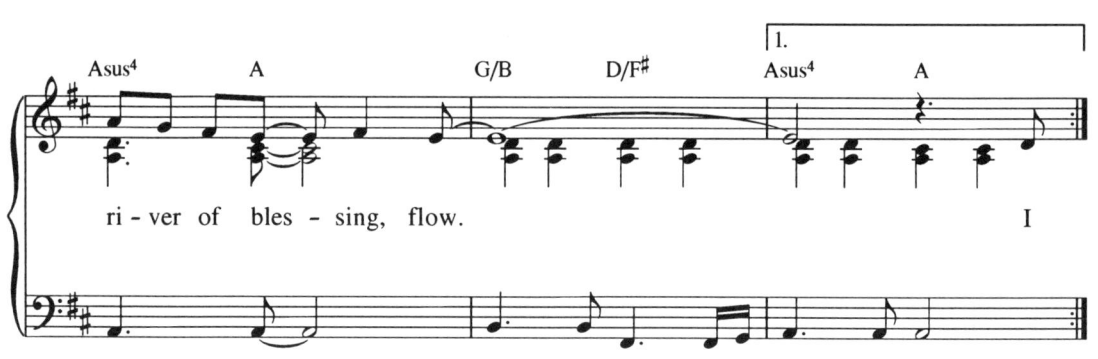

36 I lift your name
I ever will proclaim

Words and Music: Kurt Albers

© Copyright 1995 Kurt Albers. (Copyright Control).

37 I'll walk closer now
My heart will trust
Words and Music: Reuben Morgan

© Copyright 1998 Reuben Morgan/Hillsongs Publishing. Administered by Kingsway's Thankyou Music, P.O. Box 75, Eastbourne, East Sussex BN23 6NW, UK. Used by permission.

38 I'm lost for words to say
Forgiven

Words and Music: Mick Dalton

I'm lost for words to say to you, my Lord. You've
lost for words to say to you, my God. I

set me free by the pow - er of your blood.
wor - ship you from the love with - in my heart.

I'm de - clared right - eous, re - deemed by your grace; un -
Out of the dark - ness and in - to the light;

wor - thy to call you by name. All that I bring as we meet
vic - to - ry lies in your word. Healed from the past and re - stored

© Copyright 2000 Kevin Mayhew Ltd.

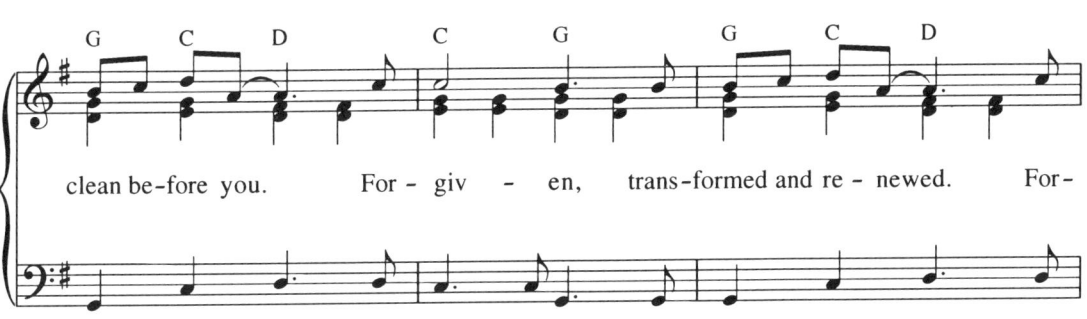

39 I'm set aside to worship you
Within your heart

Words and Music: Mick Dalton and Bonnie Davies

1. I'm set a-side to worship you,
born of the Spir-it to know your truth;
in-to your king-dom of
mer-cy and grace,
ly-ing with-in your heart.

2. You lead me be-side the qui-et stream,
gent-ly re-stor-ing my soul for me;
I've ev-'ry need, Lord, for
I'm the de-sire
ly-ing with-in your heart.

3. Ho-ly One, I lift your name,
wor-thy of hon-our I bring my praise;
stand-ing be-fore you I'm
search-ing to know the
love that's with-in your heart.

Chorus
All of your glo-ry is

© Copyright 2000 Kevin Mayhew Ltd.

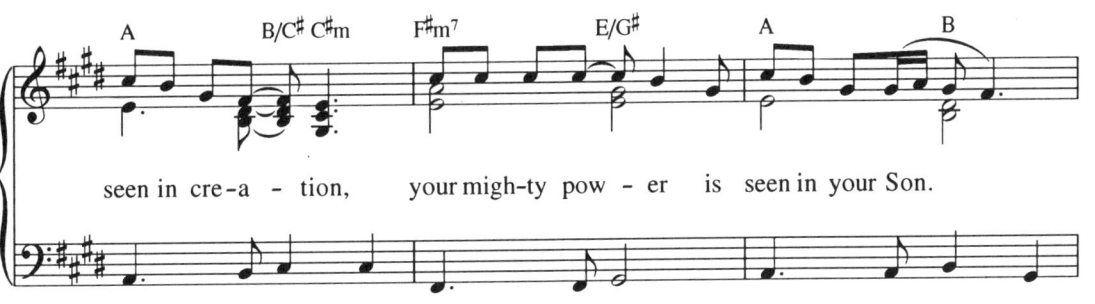

40 I need your love
Heaven

Words and Music: Reuben Morgan

© Copyright 1998 Reuben Morgan/Hillsongs Publishing. Administered by Kingsway's Thankyou Music, P.O. Box 75, Eastbourne, East Sussex BN23 6NW, UK. Used by permission.

41 In my life proclaim your glory
Lord of all mercy

Words and Music: Geoff Bullock

1. In my life proclaim your glory, in my heart reveal your majesty; then my soul shall speak the wonders of your grace, and this heart of mine shall sing your praise.

In my words proclaim your mercy, in my life reveal your power; then my soul shall be a mirror of your love, and this heart of mine shall sing your praise.

Chorus
Lord of all mercy, God of all grace, Lord of all righteousness; Lord of the heavens, Lord of the earth, enthroned in majesty.

© Copyright 1997 Watershed Productions. Administered by Kingsway's Thankyou Music,
P.O. Box 75, Eastbourne, East Sussex BN23 6NW, UK Used by permission.

2. In my soul unveil your love, Lord,
   deep within my heart, renewing me.
   Day by day, your life transforming all I am,
   as this heart of mine reflects your praise.
   Lord of all, enthroned in glory,
   grace and mercy, truth and righteousness,
   ev'ry knee shall bow before this Christ, our Lord,
   as all creation sings your praise.

43 I open my life to you
Jesus, I adore you

Words and Music: Tanya Riches

© Copyright 1998 Tanya Riches/Hillsongs Publishing. Administered by Kingsway's Thankyou Music, P.O. Box 75, Eastbourne, East Sussex BN23 6NW, UK. Used by permission.

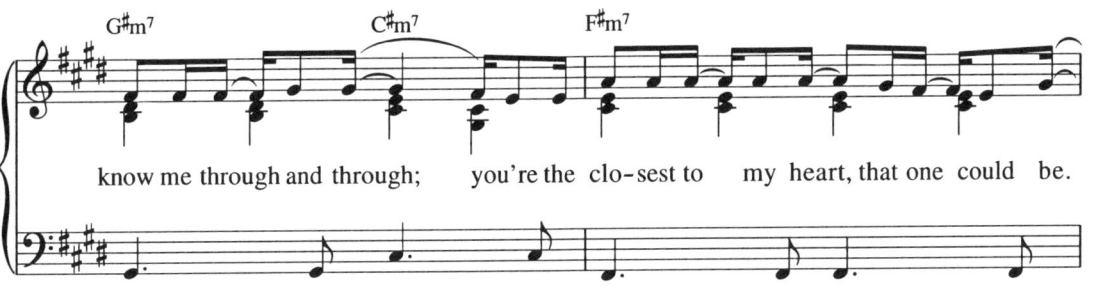

44 I see a southern land
For such a time as this

Words and Music: Colin Battersby

© Copyright 1998 Colin Battersby/Lakes Music Australia, P.O. Box 1038, Wangara, WA 6947, Australia. Used by permission.

45 I see the Lord

Words and Music: Chris Falson

© Copyright 1993 Chris Falson Music/Maranatha! Music. Administered by CopyCare, P.O. Box 77, Hailsham, East Sussex BN27 3EF, UK (music@copycare.com). Used by permission.

46 It is he

47 I've come to this house to celebrate
God is so good

Words and Music: Michael Battersby

© Copyright 1998 Michael Battersby/Smart Productions, P.O. Box 82, Victoria Park, WA 6100, Australia. Used by permission.

48 I've found the power to be free
Grateful, faithful heart
Words and Music: Russell Fragar

49 I've got joy
Unspeakable joy

Words and Music: Sam Evans

© Copyright 1998 Sam Evans/Sounds of Paradise, 2 Crowle Road, Paradise SA 5075, Australia. Used by permission.

50 I walk by faith

Words and Music: Chris Falson

© Copyright 1990 Chris Falson Music/Maranatha! Music, administered by CopyCare,
P.O. Box 77, Hailsham, East Sussex BN27 3EF, UK. Used by permission.

51 I was on your mind
On your mind

Words and Music: Mick Dalton

© Copyright 1999 Kevin Mayhew Ltd.

52 I will sing of your faithfulness
This is the day

Words and Music: Matt Poole

© Copyright 1998 Matt Poole/Sounds of Paradise, 2 Crowle Road,
Paradise SA 5075, Australia. Used by permission.

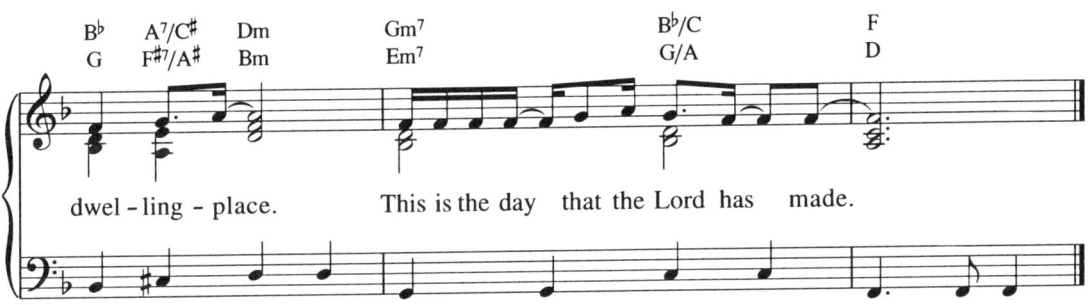

53 I will worship

© Copyright 1997 Watershed Productions. Administered by Kingsway's Thankyou Music, P.O. Box 75, Eastbourne, East Sussex BN23 6NW, UK. Used by permission.

54 Jesus, I need you
In your likeness

Words and Music: Colin Battersby and Kristian Anderson

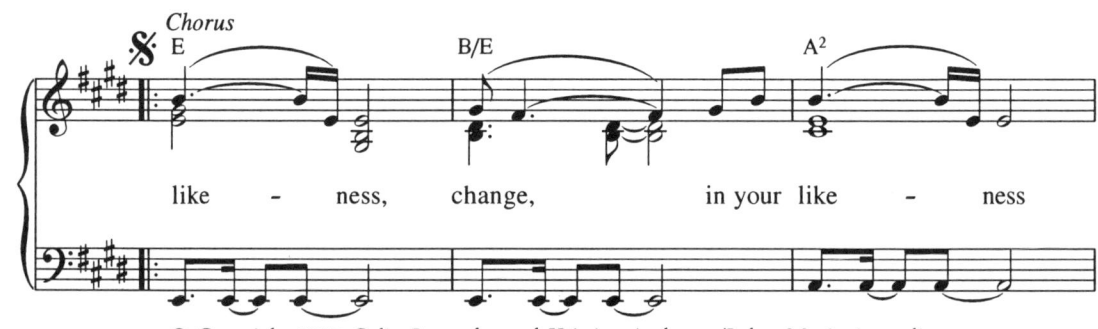

© Copyright 1997 Colin Battersby and Kristian Anderson/Lakes Music Australia,
P.O. Box 1038, Wangara, WA 6947, Australia. Used by permission.

55 Jesus, Jesus you are the one
Jesus, Holy One of God

Words and Music: Michael Battersby

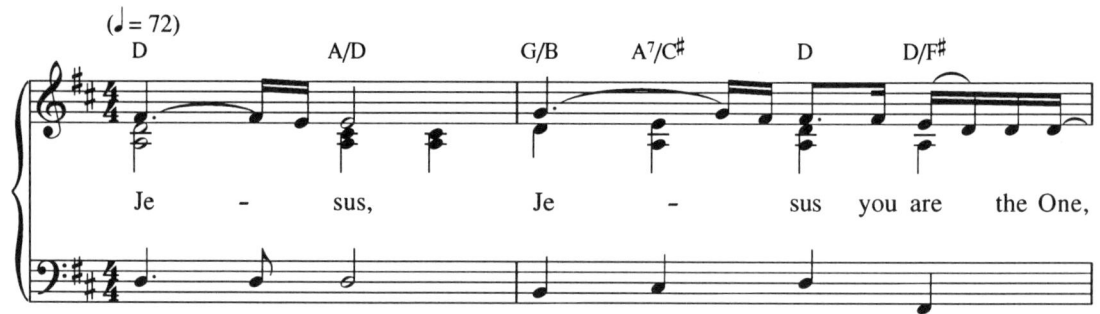

© Copyright 1996 Michael Battersby/Smart Productions, P.O. Box 82, Victoria Park, WA 6100, Australia. Used by permission.

56 Jesus, no one loves me more
No name like Jesus

Words and Music: Sam Tzeegenkoff

© Copyright 1996 Sam Tzeegenkoff. (Copyright Control)

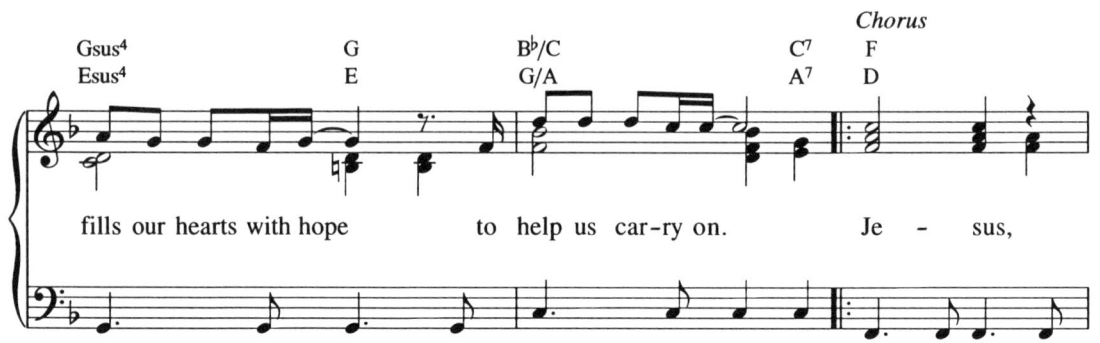
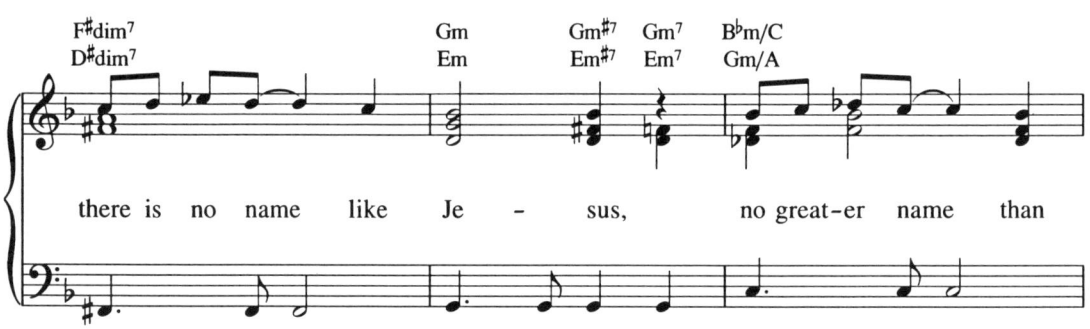

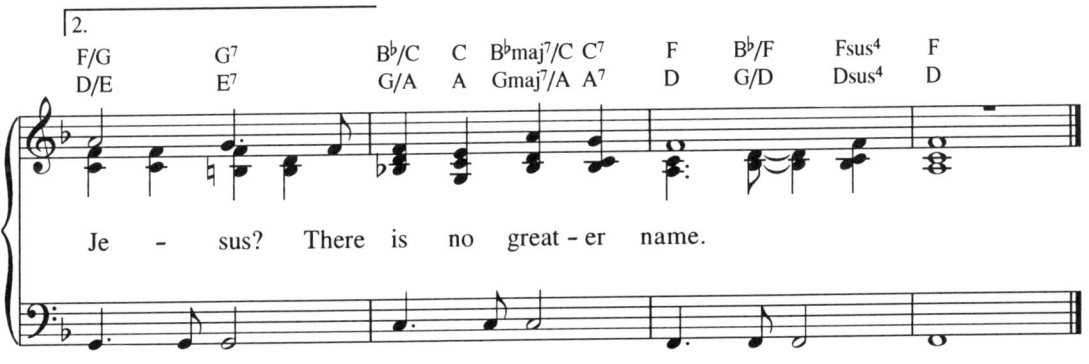

Kingdoms will come
Let it be known

Words and Music: David Evans

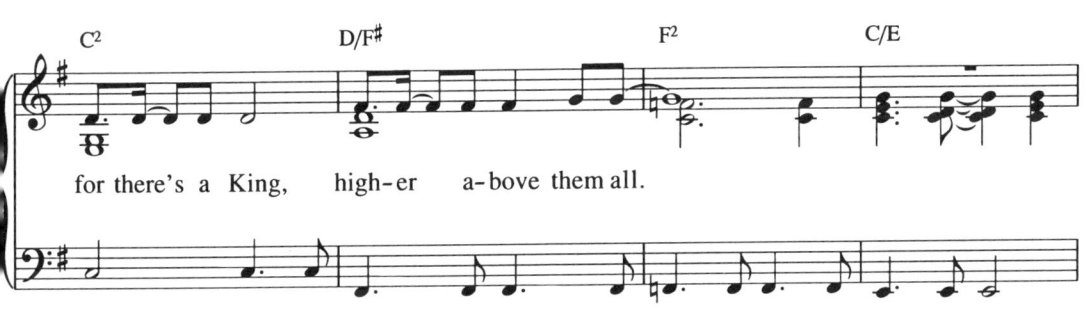

© Copyright 1996 Heartfelt Music, 84 Sherry Street,
Carseldine, QLD 4034, Australia. Used by permission.

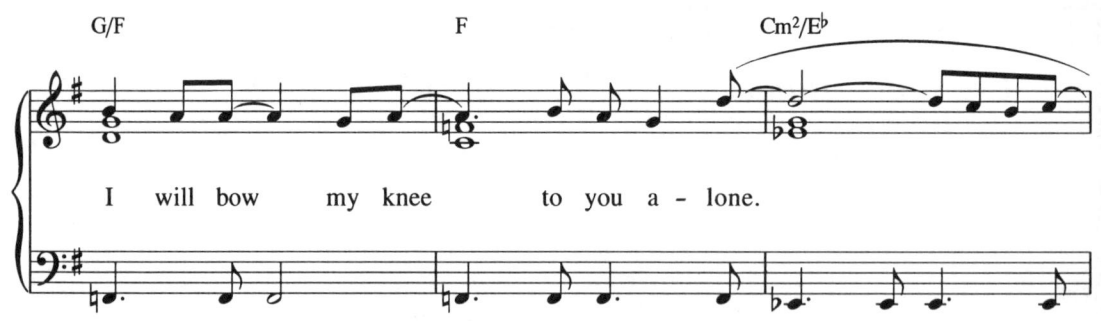

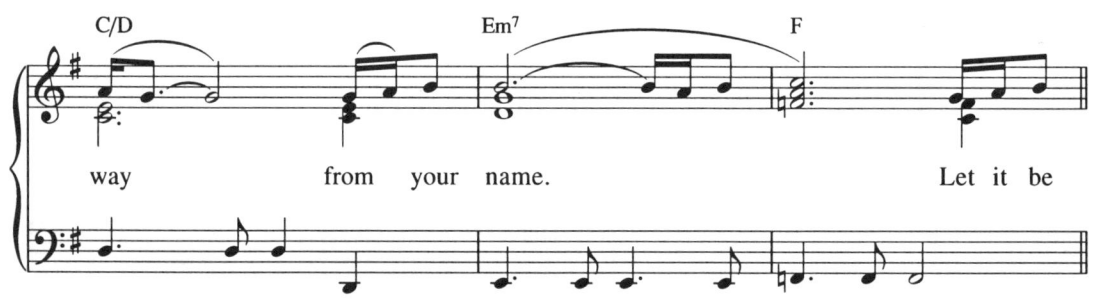

58 Let there be joy

Words and Music: Bruce Napier

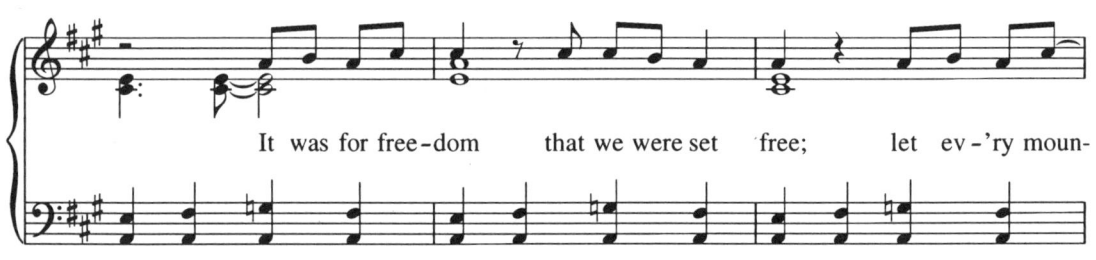

© Copyright 1996 Ironspiration Music, P.O. Box 228, Woombye,
Queensland 4559, Australia. Used by permission.

59 Let the weak say I am strong
What the Lord has done in me

Words and Music: Reuben Morgan

© Copyright 1998 Reuben Morgan/Hillsongs Publishing. Administered by Kingsway's Thankyou Music, P.O. Box 75, Eastbourne, East Sussex BN23 6NW, UK. Used by permission.

60 Let your glory

Words and Music: Russell Evans

© Copyright 1996 Russell Evans/Sounds of Paradise, 2 Crowle Road,
Paradise SA 5075, Australia. Used by permission.

61 Let your Spirit come

Words and Music: Graham Paull

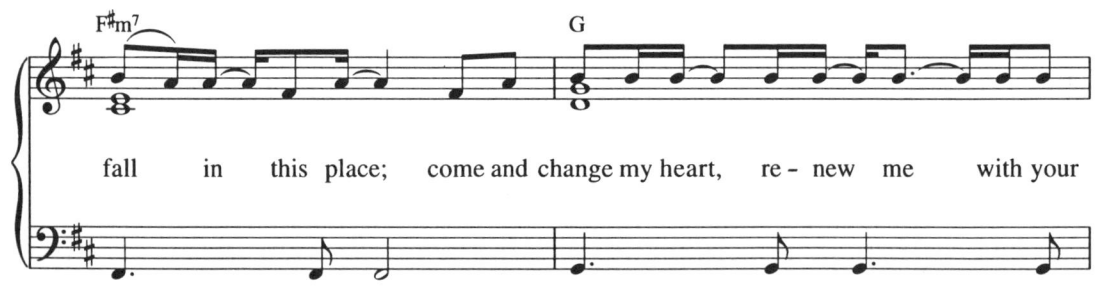

© Copyright 1998 Graham Paull/Sounds of Paradise, 2 Crowle Road,
Paradise SA 5057, Australia. Used by permission.

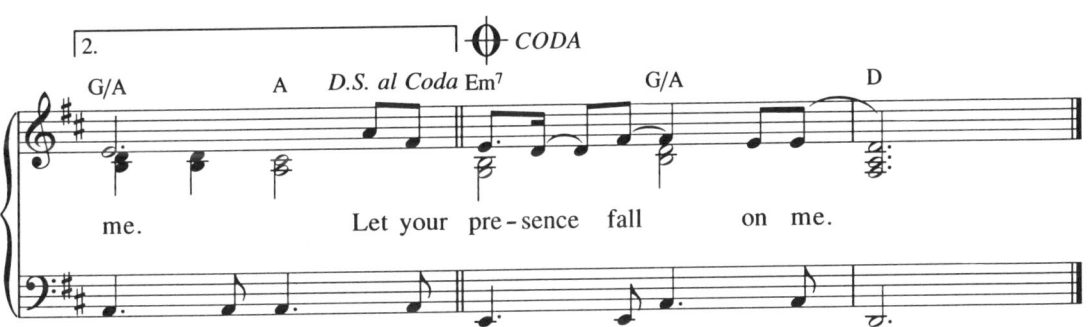

2. Healed and whole in our brokenness
   our pieces held in the master's hands.
   When all is lost the lost are found
   life comes to us in Jesus' crown.

3. Love has come to our loveless lives,
   light has filled our endless night.
   Filled with peace in grace we're found,
   love overthrows through Jesus' crown.

63 Lord of creation
In your presence
Words and Music: Mick Dalton

© Copyright 1999 Kevin Mayhew Ltd.

64 Lord, to serve you is my joy
You shine

Words and Music: Russell Fragar

© Copyright 1998 Russell Fragar/Hillsongs Publishing. Administered by Kingsway's Thankyou Music, P.O. Box 75, Eastbourne, East Sussex BN23 6NW, UK. Used by permission.

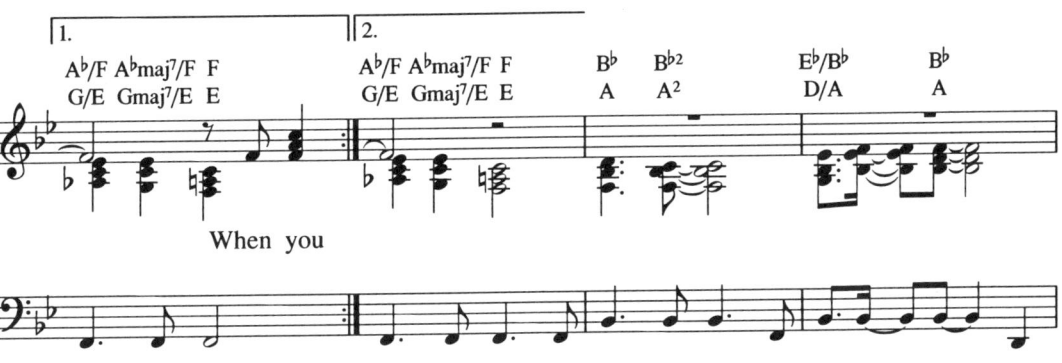

65 Lord, you are my solid ground
You arrested me

Words and Music: Mick Dalton

© Copyright 2000 Kevin Mayhew Ltd.

66 Lord, you are the one
Yet will I praise thee

Words and Music: Glenn 'Henry' Seeley

© Copyright 1998 Manic Productions, 2 Crowle Road, Paradise, South Australia 5075

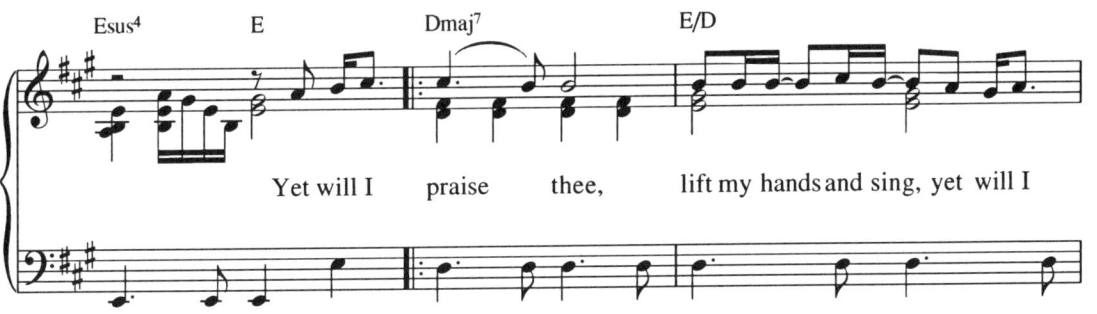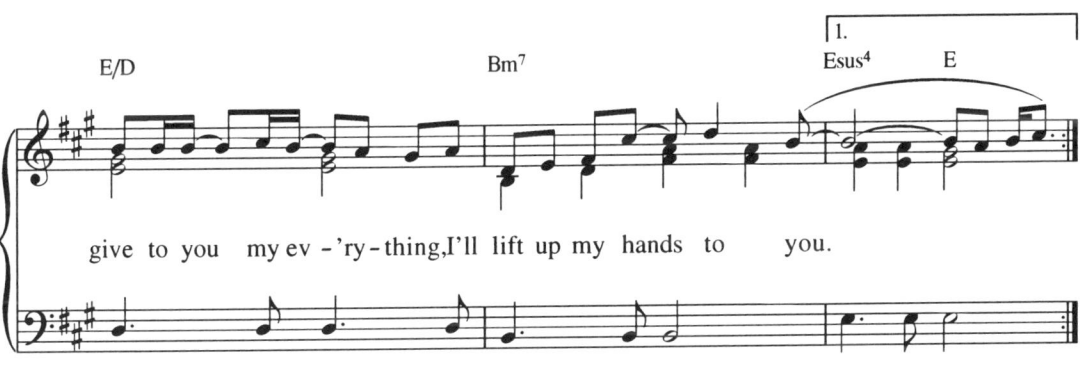

67 Lovely are your dwelling-places
Dwelling-places

Words and Music: Miriam Webster

© Copyright 1999 Miriam Webster/Hillsongs Publishing. Administered by Kingsway's Thankyou Music, P.O. Box 75, Eastbourne, East Sussex BN23 6NW, UK. Used by permission.

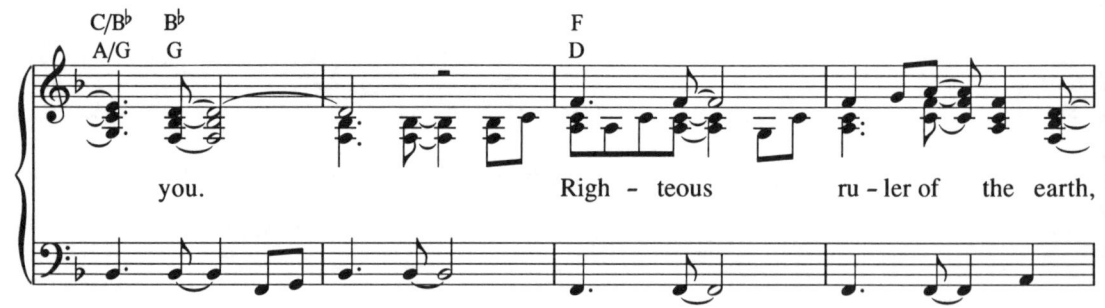
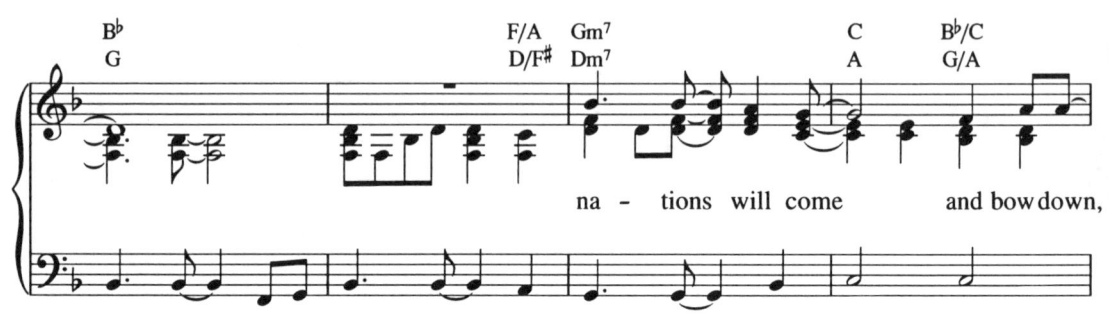

68 May our homes be filled with dancing
Hear our praises

Words and Music: Reuben Morgan

1. May our homes be filled with danc-ing,
2. May our light shine in the dark-ness,

may our streets be filled with joy;
as we walk be-fore the cross;

may in-jus-tice bow to Je-sus
may your glo - ry fill the whole earth

as the peo - ple turn and pray. From the
as the wa - ter o'er the seas.

© Copyright 1998 Reuben Morgan/Hillsongs Publishing/Kingsway's Thankyou Music,
P.O. Box 75, Eastbourne, East Sussex BN23 6NW, UK. Used by permission.

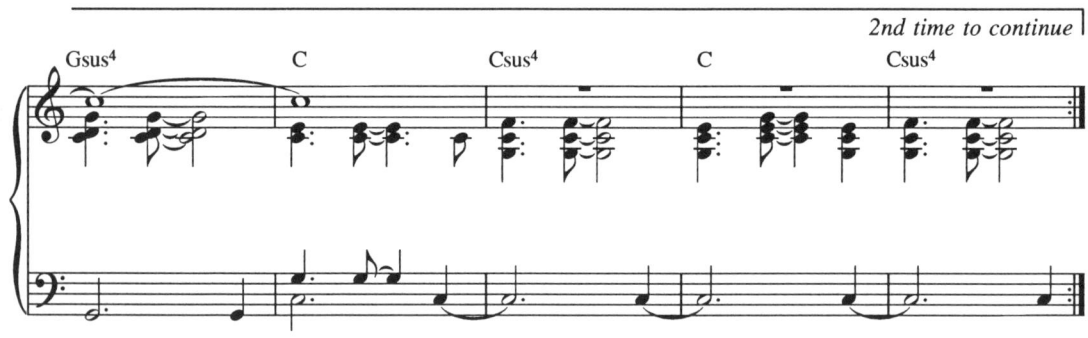

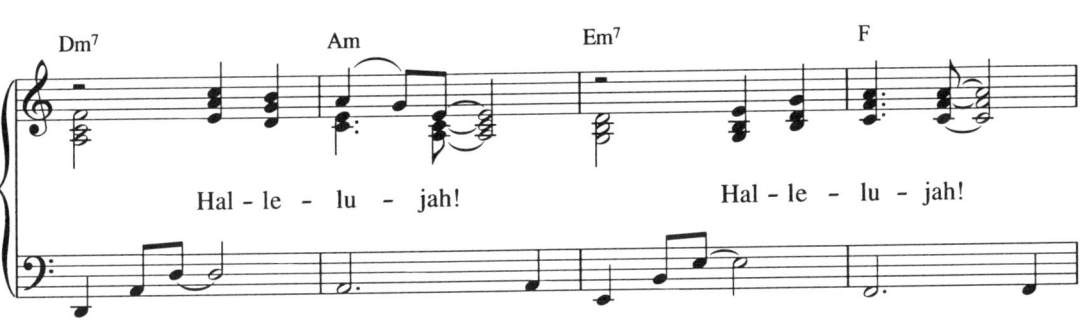

69 Never to be alone
Light to blinded eyes

Words and Music: Geoff Bullock

1. Never to be alone, never again to roam; lonely in darkest night, life is now filled with light. Never again to fear the perfect way draws near to still the anxious soul 'til I am healed and whole.

Chorus
Oh, light to blinded eyes, oh,

© Copyright 1999 Watershed Productions. Administered by Kingsway's Thankyou Music,
P.O. Box 75, Eastbourne, East Sussex BN23 6NW, UK. Used by permission.

2. Paths I once strayed at night
   have become paved with light.
   Light that once made me fear,
   light that now draws me near.
   Light that now makes me see,
   life that has set me free;
   free in the darkest night
   life is now filled with light.

3. Never to be afraid,
   love has destroyed the chains.
   Chains that had held me bound,
   broken when I was found.
   Bound by your perfect light,
   light that restored my sight;
   eyes that are healed by grace,
   eyes that now see your face.

70 No higher place

Words and Music: Geoff Bullock

© Copyright 1999 Watershed Productions. Administered by Kingsway's Thankyou Music,
P.O. Box 75, Eastbourne, East Sussex BN23 6NW, UK. Used by permission.

2. This place of love from the moment I was found,
   the hope of life, my heavy soul's release.
   You freed my heart to soar on wings of love;
   this place of love, no higher place.

3. No higher place where all I see is you,
   this gift of grace that covers all I do.
   Grace compels me now to soar on wings of love;
   no higher place, no higher place.

71 O dear God
By your side

Words and Music: Marty Sampson

© Copyright 1999 Marty Sampson/Hillsongs Publishing. Administered by Kingsway's Thankyou Music, P.O. Box 75, Eastbourne, East Sussex BN23 6NW, UK. Used by permission.

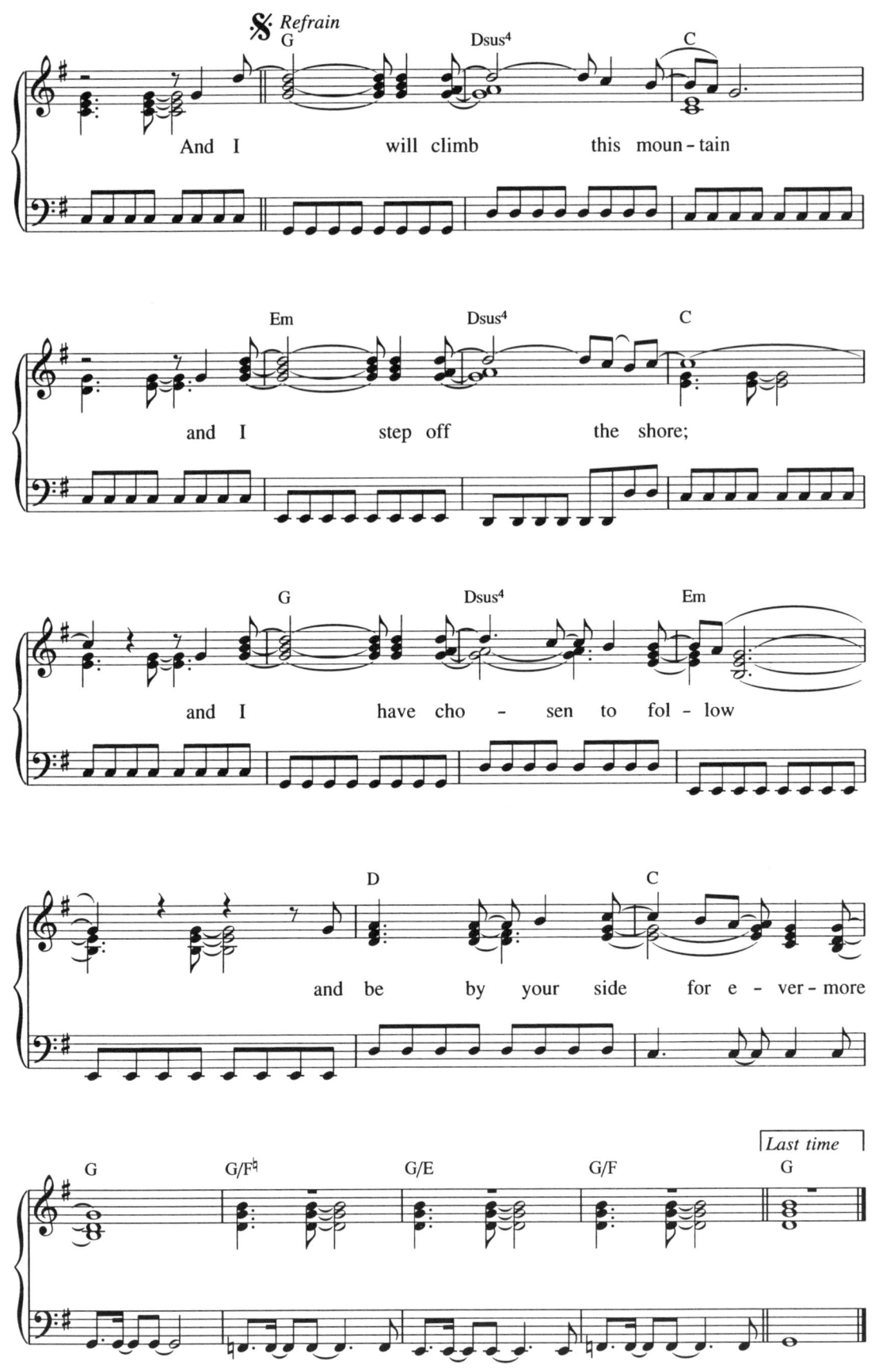

72 O God of my comfort

Words and Music: Geoff Bullock

1. O God of my comfort, O God of my strength; Lord God of all wisdom, sweet Lord of my peace. Bright light in the darkness, soft voice in the night; O God, my assurance, my way and my life. *(Chorus)* O God, my joy. O God, my

© Copyright 1997 Watershed Productions. Administered by Kingsway's Thankyou Music,
P.O. Box 75, Eastbourne, East Sussex BN23 6NW, UK. Used by permission.

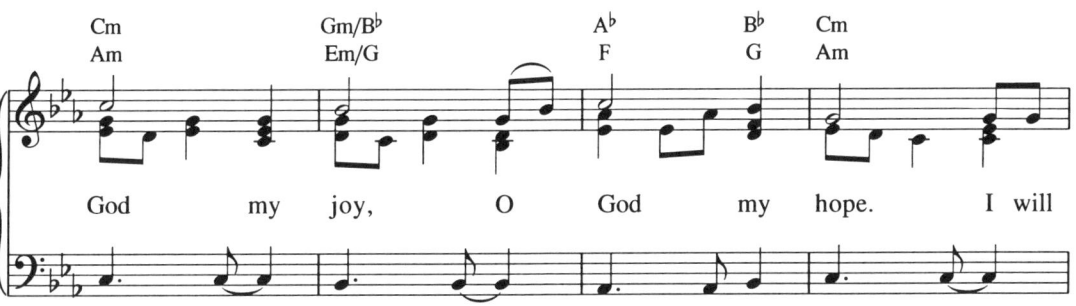
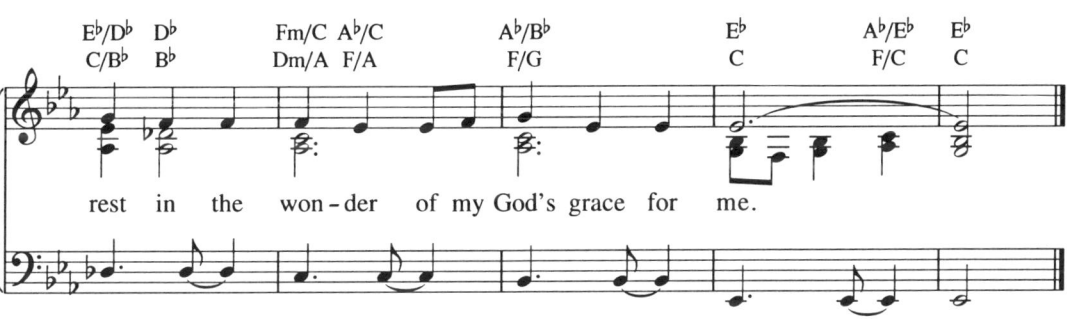

2. O God who brings comfort,
   O God who sends grace;
   grace for the weary and mercy for me.
   Who heals and restores like the sun and the rain
   to soften these dark wounds,
   to bring life again.

3. O God who in mercy has seen every pain,
   who gently speaks words that heal hope again.
   O God, Lord of heaven
   embraced this earth's lost
   to bring home the homeless
   and pay sin's cruel cost.

73 O Lord, you're amazing
I'm here to worship you

Words and Music: Michael Battersby

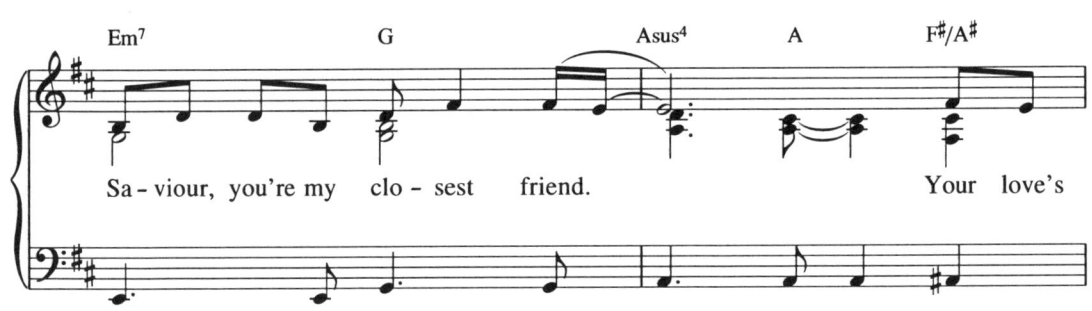

© Copyright 1997 Michael Battersby/Smart Productions, P.O. Box 82,
Victoria Park, WA 6100, Australia. Used by permission.

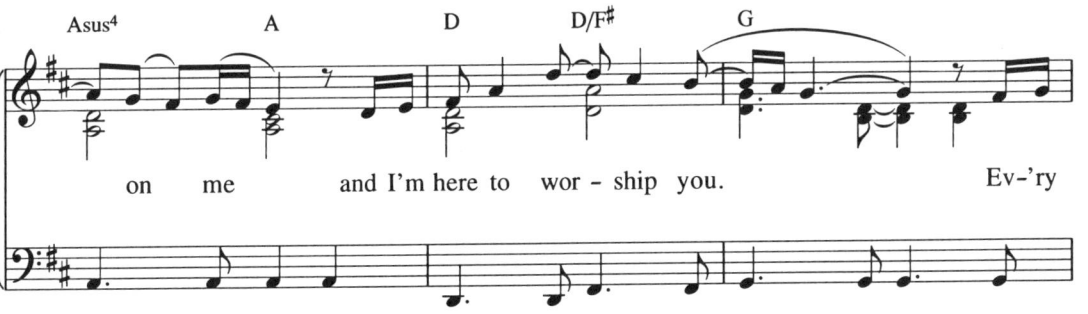

74 Praise him, you heavens
Great in power

Words and Music: Russell Fragar

© Copyright 1998 Hillsongs Publishing/Kingsway's Thankyou Music, P.O. Box 75, Eastbourne, East Sussex BN23 6NW, UK. Used by permission.

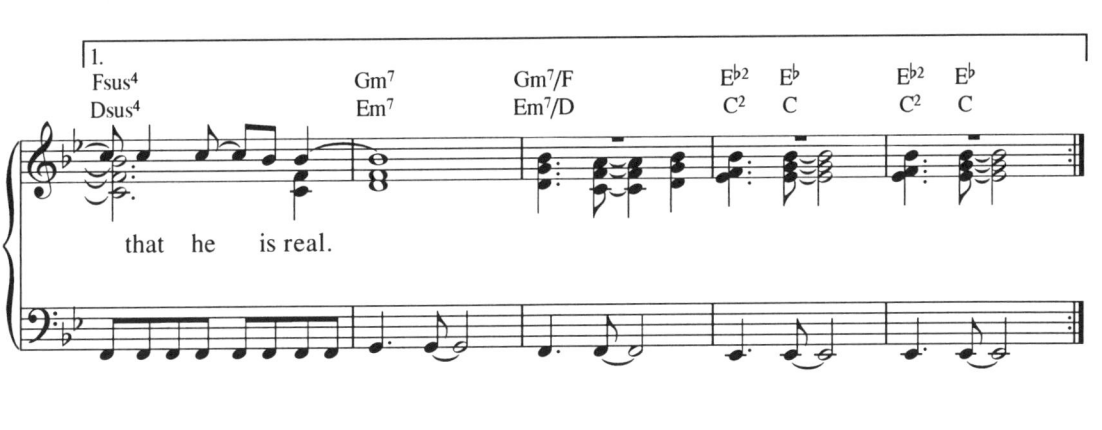

76 Surely goodness

Words and Music: Colin Battersby

© Copyright 1999 Colin Battersby/Lakes Music Australia, P.O. Box 1038, Wangara, WA 6947, Australia. Used by permission.

77 There is a sound of great rejoicing
Make a way

Words and Music: Michael Battersby

© Copyright 1998 Michael Battersby/Smart Productions, P.O. Box 82,
Victoria Park, WA 6100, Australia. Used by permission.

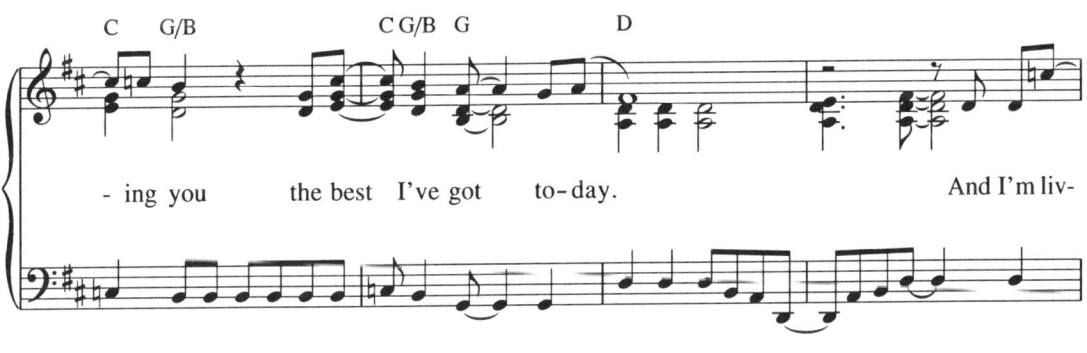
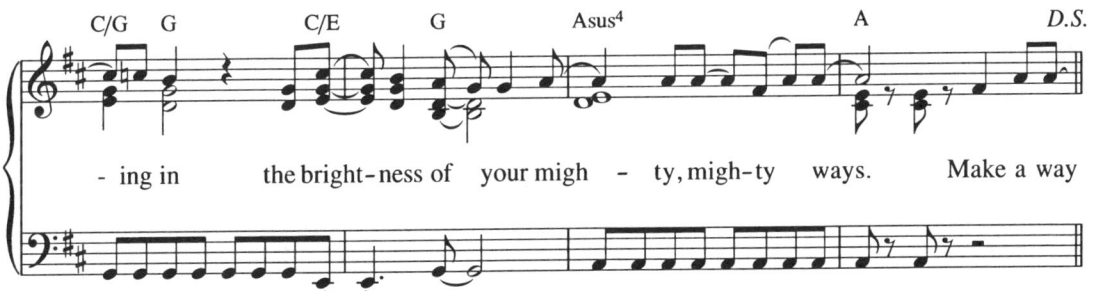

78 There is hope beyond

Mercy

Words and Music: Geoff Bullock

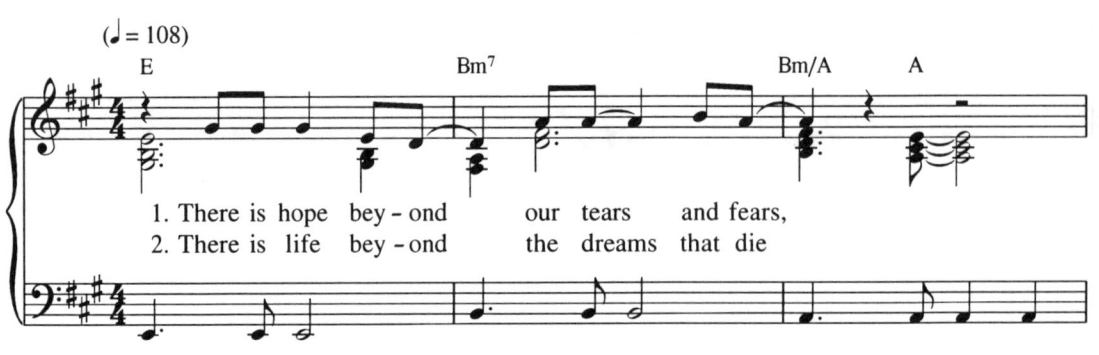

1. There is hope beyond our tears and fears,
2. There is life beyond the dreams that die

there is dawn that comes to break the
where hope will rise in life de-

deep-est dark-est night. As light now floods the dark
fy-ing ev-'ry fear. As beau-ty comes to ash-

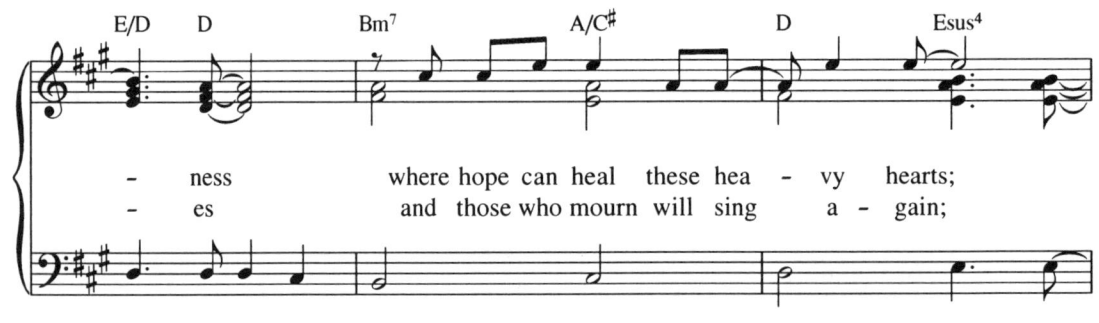

-ness where hope can heal these hea-vy hearts;
-es and those who mourn will sing a-gain;

© Copyright 1999 Watershed Productions. Administered by Kingsway's Thankyou Music,
P.O. Box 75, Eastbourne, East Sussex BN23 6NW. For the UK only. Used by permission.

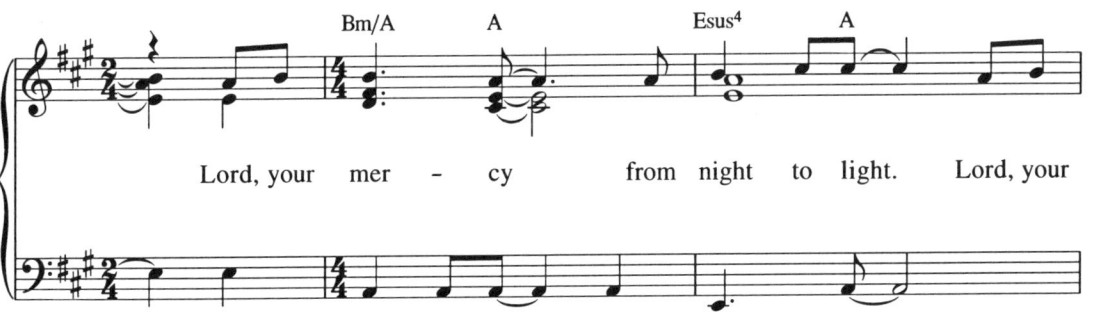

79 There is no other name
No other name

Words and Music: Colin Battersby

There is no other name by which we can be saved,
there is no other name like Jesus.
You give me joy, you give me peace, you set my Spirit free,
You lift me up to higher ground, you're all I need. I'm gonna
praise you all my days, I'm gonna follow you, there's no

© Copyright 1999 Colin Battersby/Lakes Music Australia, P.O. Box 1038,
Wangara, WA 6947, Australia. Used by permission.

80 There's a party goin' on

Words and Music: Andrew Ironside

There's a par-ty go-in' on to-night, some-one's just been born a-gain.

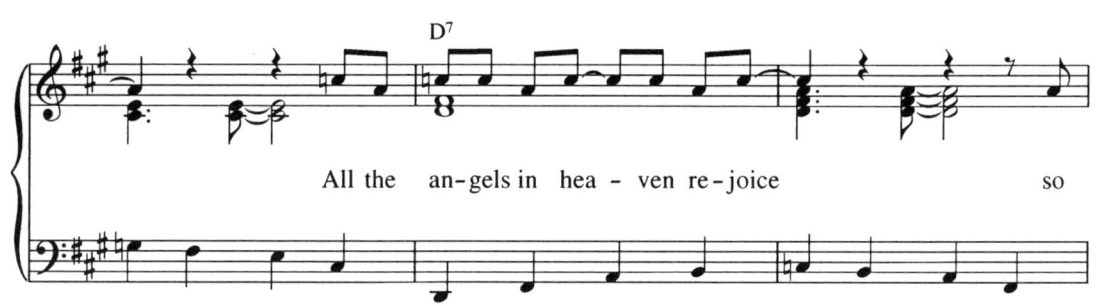

All the an-gels in hea-ven re-joice so

come on and lift your voice, there'll be danc-ing a-round the throne

as one more sin-ner comes home. There's a

© Copyright 1997 Ironspiration Music, P.O. Box 228, Woombye,
Queensland 4559, Australia. Used by permission.

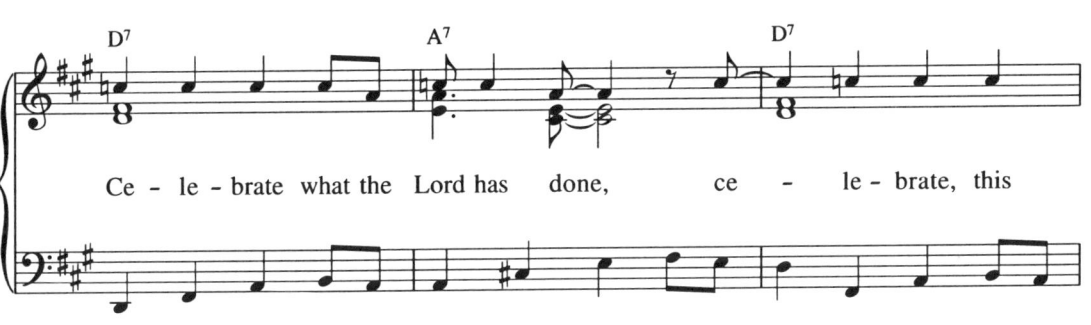
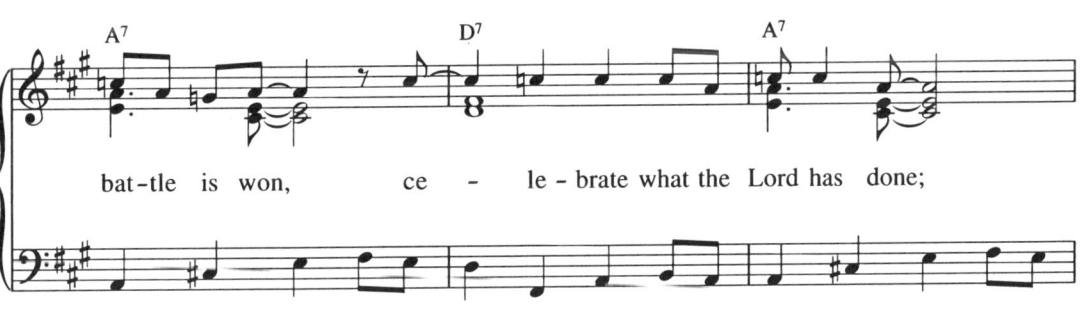

81 The Spirit of the Lord

Words and Music: Andrew and Desma Ironside

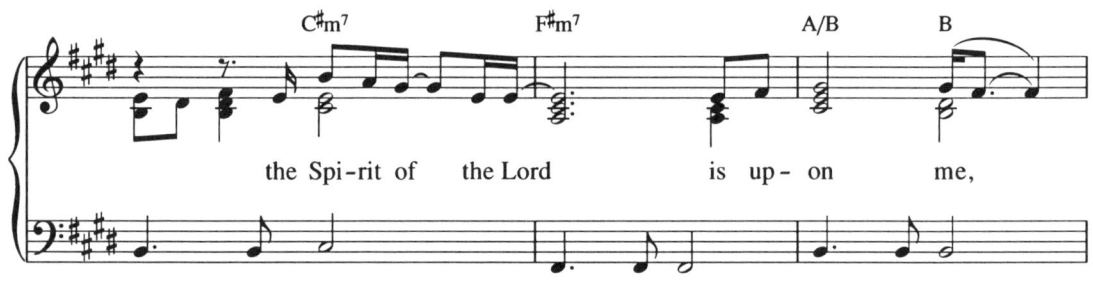

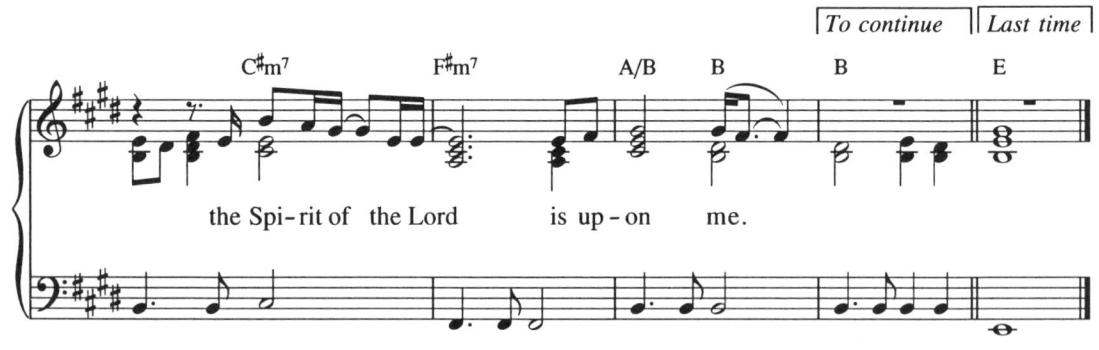

© Copyright 1997 Ironspiration Music, P.O. Box 226, Woombye,
Queensland 4559, Australia. Used by permission.

82 The steadfast love of the Lord

Words and Music: John and Donia Makedonez

© Copyright 1998 John and Donia Makedonez/Hillsongs Publishing. Administered by Kingsway's Thankyou Music, P.O. Box 75, Eastbourne, East Sussex BN23 6NW, UK. Used by permission.

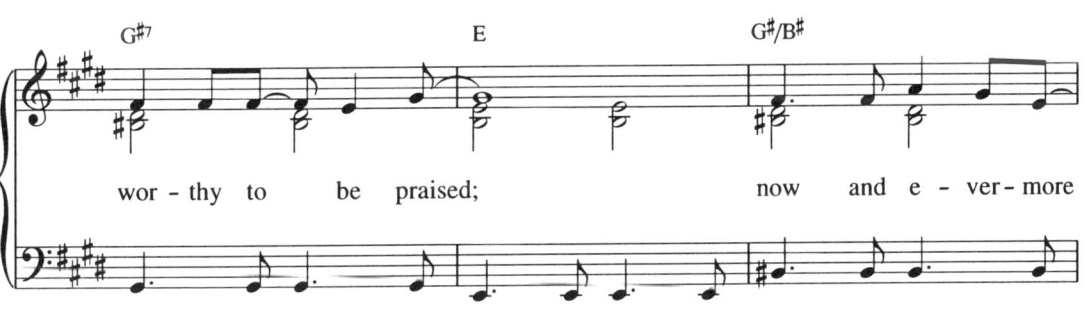
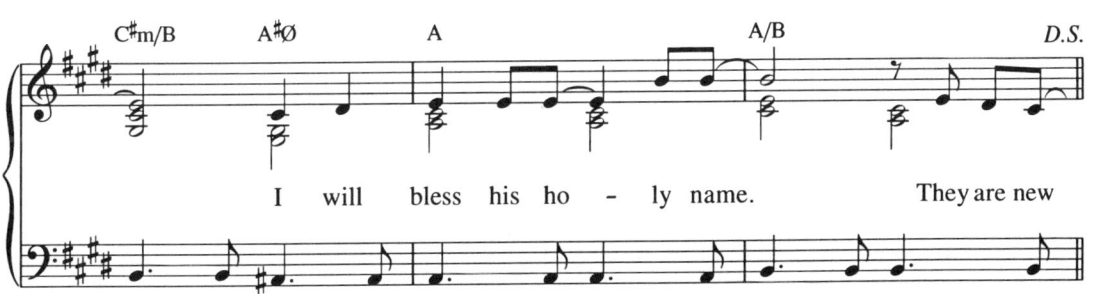

83 This is the sound of a warrior
Sound of a warrior

Words and Music: Andrew Ironside and Condy Canuto

This is the sound of a war-ri-or march-ing to the beat of a

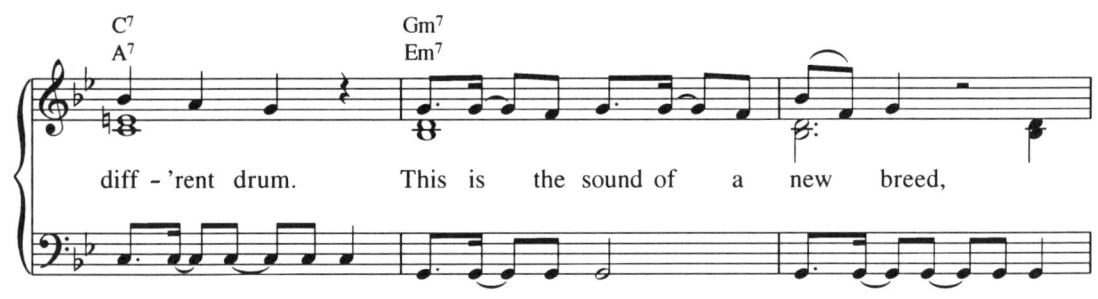
diff-'rent drum. This is the sound of a new breed,

stomp-in' on the head of the e-vil one. This is the sound of de-

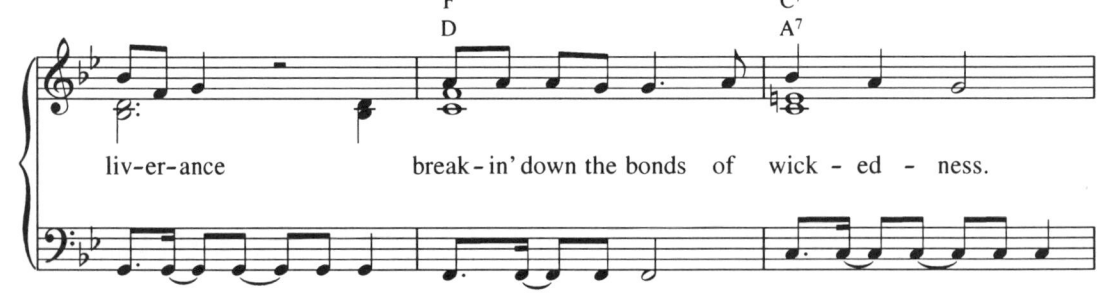
liv-er-ance break-in' down the bonds of wick-ed-ness.

© Copyright 1998 Ironspiration Music, P.O. Box 228, Woombye,
Queensland 4559, Australia. Used by permission.

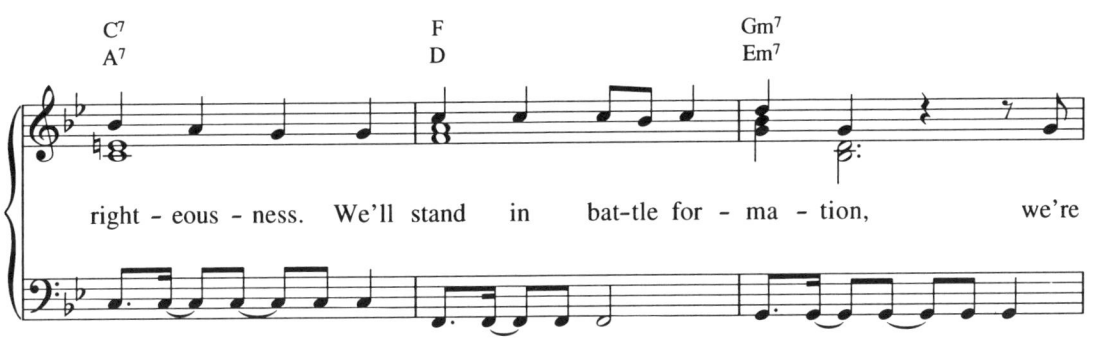

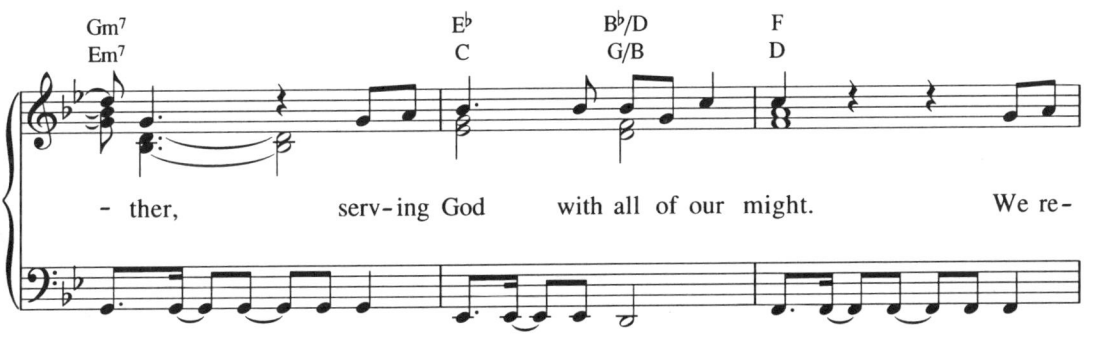

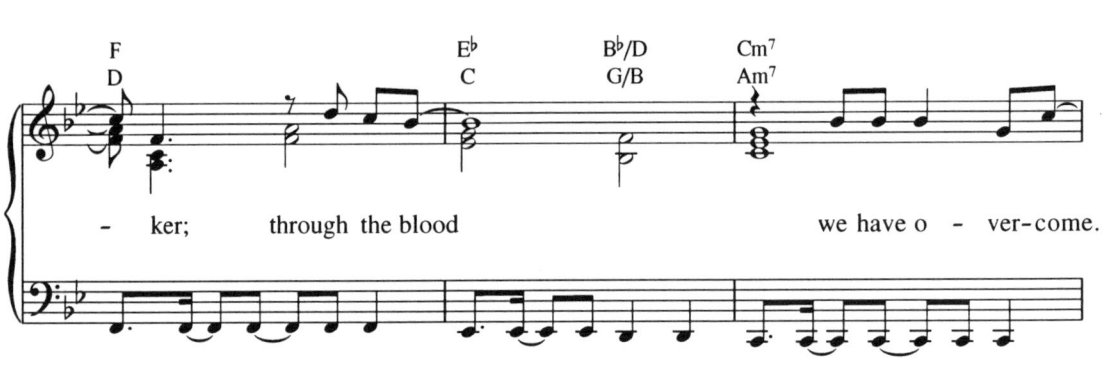

84 This song in my heart
Free to dance

Words and Music: Darlene Zschech

This song in my heart, this song in my soul, this song I was born to sing:

it's your song of free-dom, now I'm free to dance a-gain.

I'll sing in the dark-ness, I'll

laugh in the rain, re-joice in your love a-gain. It's your song of

© Copyright 1999 Darlene Zschech/Hillsongs Publishing. Administered by Kingsway's Thankyou Music, P.O. Box 75, Eastbourne, East Sussex BN23 6NW, UK. Used by permission.

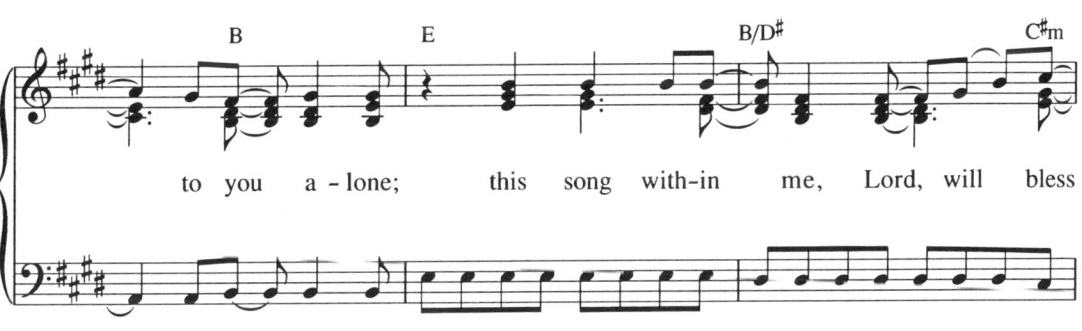

85 This yearning deep within me
Have your way

Words and Music: Darlene Zschech

© Copyright 1998 Hillsongs Publishing/Kingsway's Thankyou Music, P.O. Box 75, Eastbourne, East Sussex BN23 6NW, UK. Used by permission.

86 We come into your presence
That's what we came here for

Words and Music: Russell Fragar and Darlene Zschech

© Copyright 1997 Hillsongs Publishing. Administered by Kingsway's Thankyou Music, P.O. Box 75, Eastbourne, East Sussex BN23 6NW, UK. Used by permission.

87 We have a vision

Words and Music: Chris Falson

We have a vision for this nation,

we share a dream for this land,

we join with angels

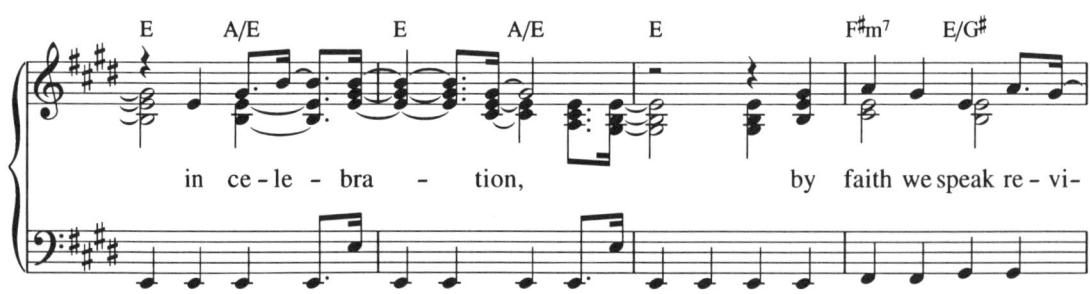
in celebration, by faith we speak re-vi-

© Copyright 1990 Chris Falson Music. Administered by Kingsway's Thankyou Music, P.O. Box 75, Eastbourne, East Sussex BN23 6NW, UK. For the UK territory only. Used by permission.

88 Well, we've come to this house
Your glory

Words and Music: David Evans, Glenn Seeley and Luke Anderson

© Copyright Heartfelt Music/Manic Productions/Luke Anderson.
Used by permission.

89 We will never be the same

Words and Music: Michael Battersby

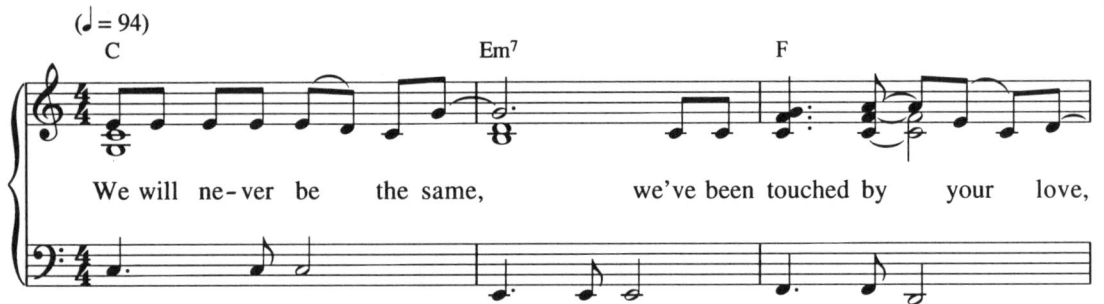

We will ne-ver be the same, we've been touched by your love,

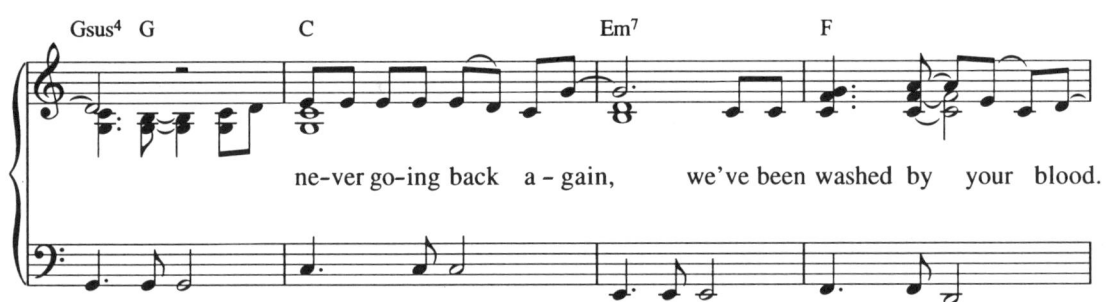

ne-ver go-ing back a-gain, we've been washed by your blood.

Deep calls, deep calls to deep,

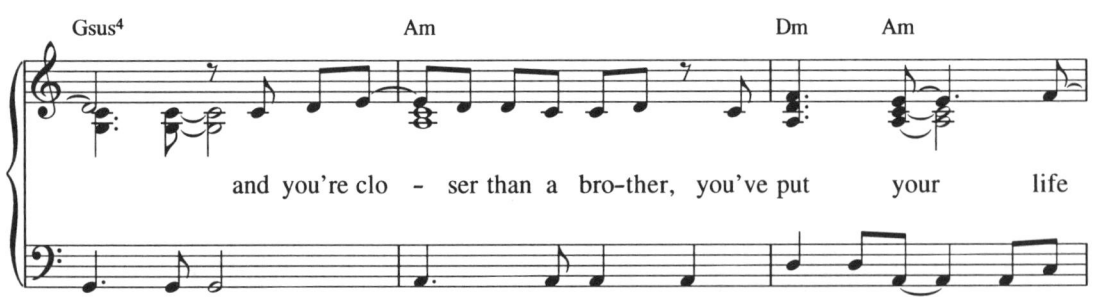

and you're clo - ser than a bro-ther, you've put your life

© Copyright 1996 Michael Battersby/Smart Productions, P.O. Box 82,
Victoria Park, WA 6100, Australia. Used by permission.

90 When I feel you near

Words and Music: Guy Sebastian and Oliver Sebastian

© Copyright 1997 Guy Sebastian and Oliver Sebastian/Sounds of Paradise, 2 Crowle Road, Paradise SA 5075, Australia. Used by permission.

91 When the darkness fills my senses
Your unfailing love

Words and Music: Reuben Morgan

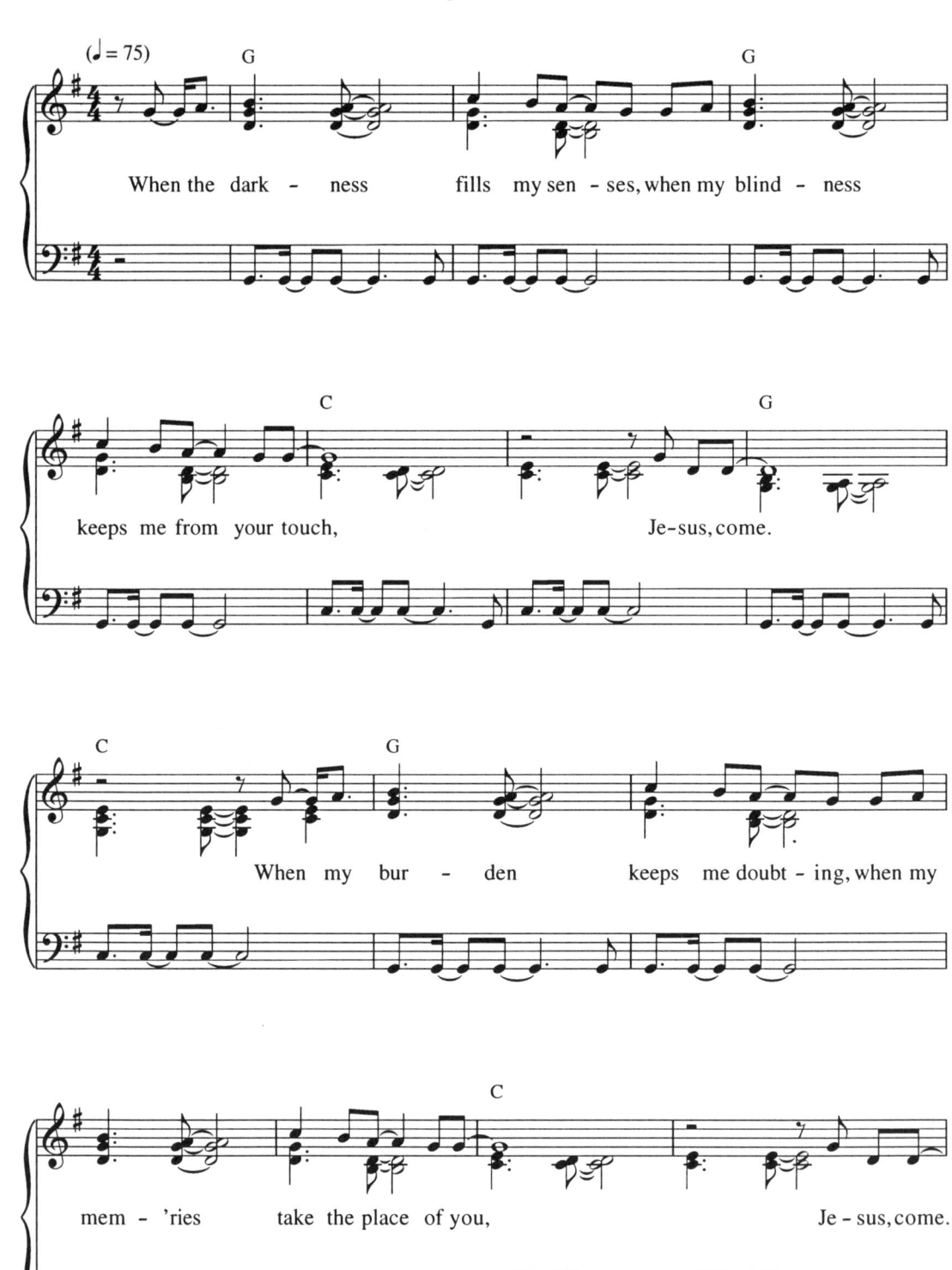

© Copyright 1998 Reuben Morgan/Hillsongs Publishing. Administered by Kingsway's Thankyou Music, P.O. Box 75, Eastbourne, East Sussex BN23 6NW, UK. Used by permission.

92 Within my heart
Touch me with your love

Words and Music: Mick Dalton and Bonnie Davies

1. With-in my heart I feel your pre - sence,
(2.) -in my heart I feel your com - fort,

teach-ing me now to ne-ver let go.
you let me know your kind of love.

You hear me when I call your name,
Ris-ing from in my si - lent place,

Je - sus my Lord, my friend, my King, hold me now,
you give me grace to see your face, hold me now,

© Copyright 2000 Kevin Mayhew Ltd.

93 You are a strong and firm foundation
Glorified

Words and Music: Steve McPherson

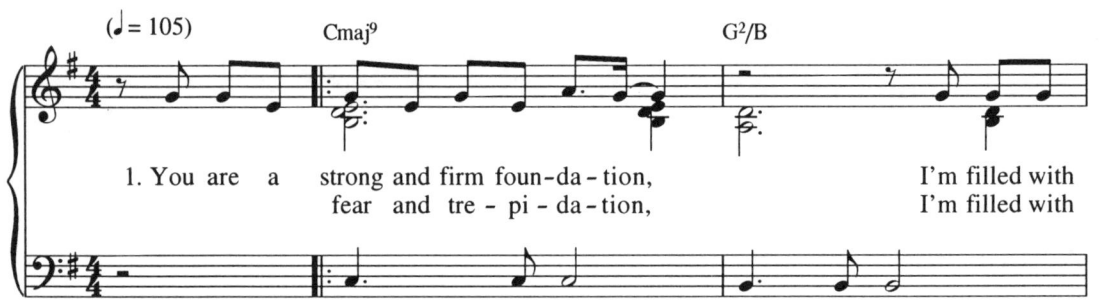

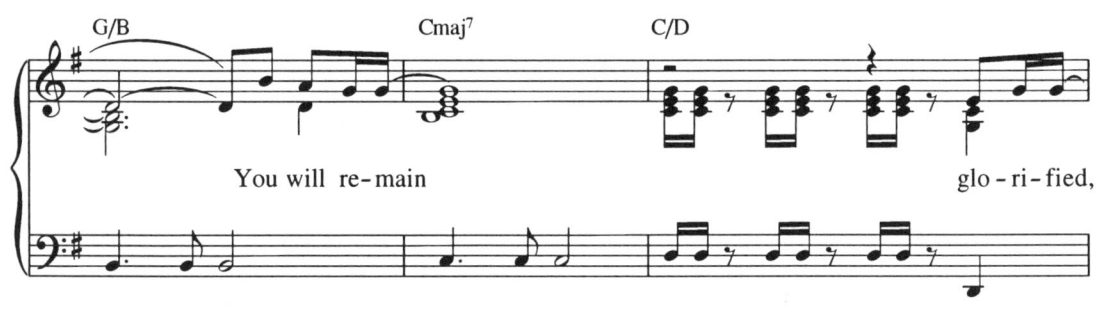

© Copyright 1997 Steve McPherson/Hillsongs Publishing. Administered by Kingsway's Thankyou Music, P.O. Box 75, Eastbourne, East Sussex BN23 6NW, UK. Used by permission.

94 You are high and lifted up
Grace and mercy

Words and Music: Andrew and Desme Ironside

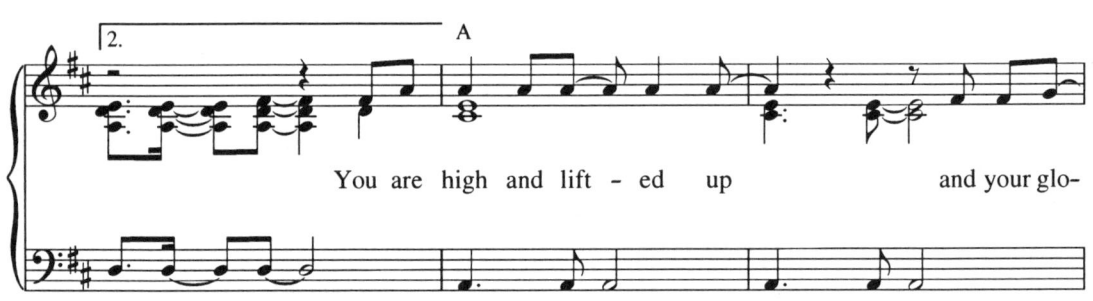

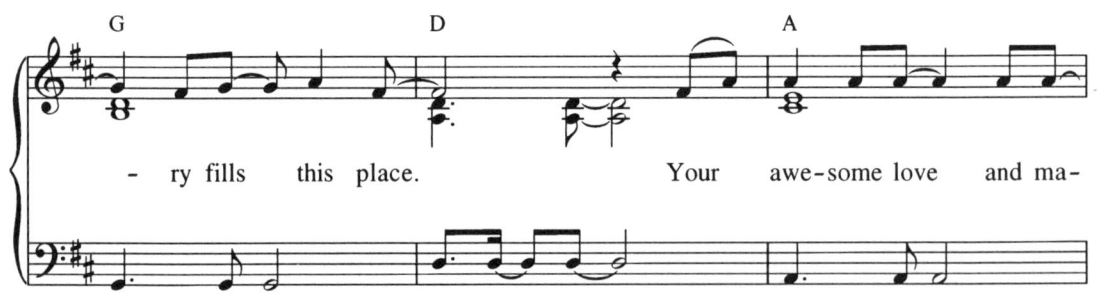

© Copyright 1997 Ironspiration Music, P.O. Box 228, Woombye, Queensland 4559, Australia. Used by permission.

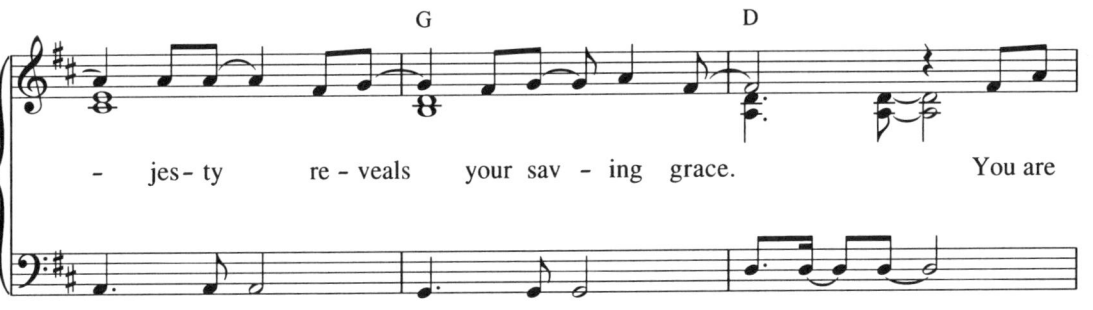
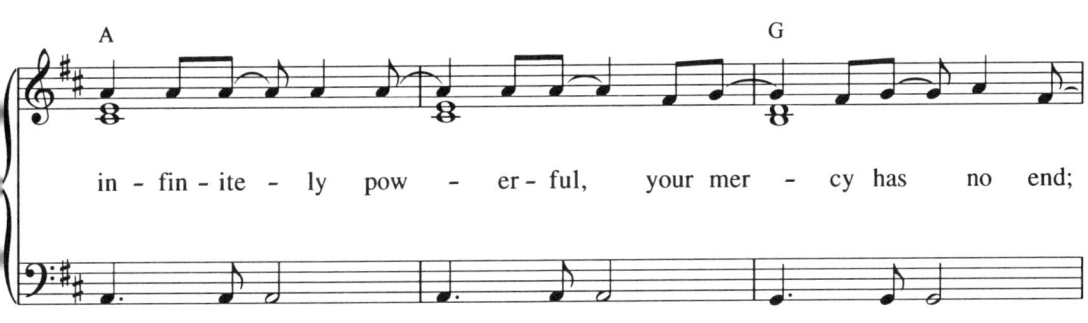

95 You are so faithful
The only one

Words and Music: Mick Dalton

© Copyright 2000 Kevin Mayhew Ltd.

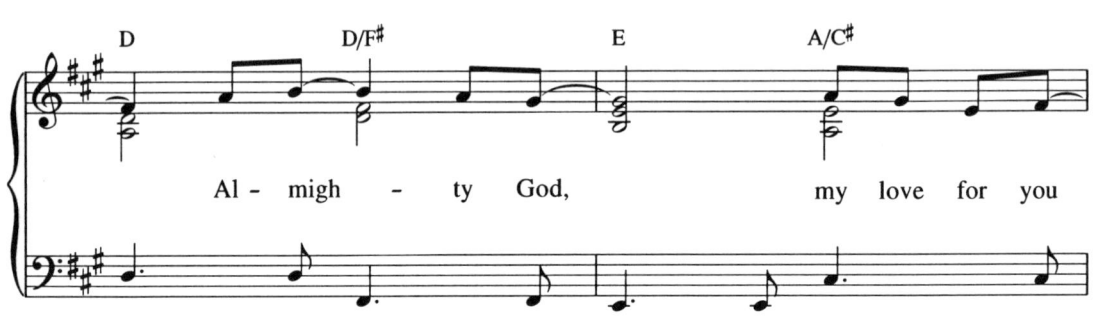
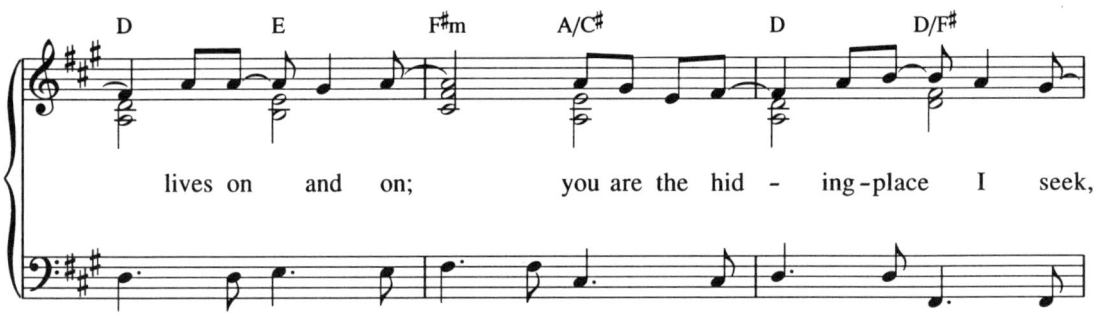

96 You gave me a love

Words and Music: Reuben Morgan

1. You gave me a love that caused my heart to o-ver-flow,
2. You gave me a love of-fered my life a brand new start,

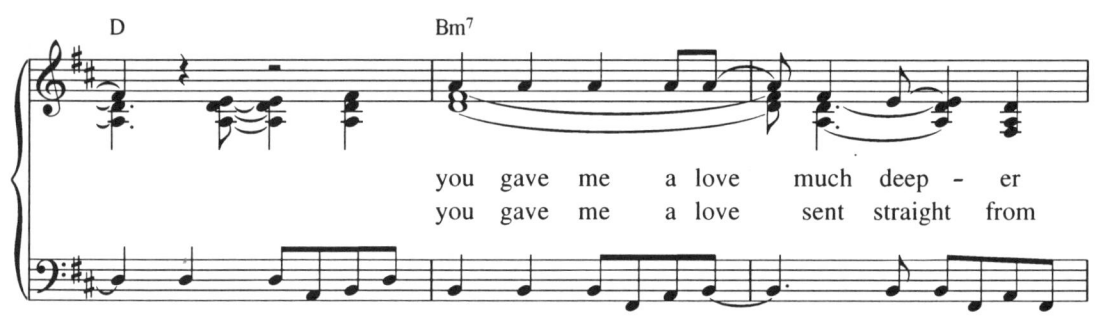

1. you gave me a love much deep-er
2. you gave me a love sent straight from

1. than I've e-ver known,
2. hea-ven to my heart,

you have set my feet
fur-ther than the east

1. where I be-long,
2. is from the west.

You've

© Copyright 1997 Reuben Morgan/Hillsongs Publishing. Administered by Kingsway's Thankyou Music, P.O. Box 75, Eastbourne, East Sussex BN23 6NW, UK. Used by permission.

97 You're the light of my world
All is well

Words and Music: Mick Dalton

© Copyright 2000 Kevin Mayhew Ltd.

3. To the glory of God salvation has come,
   so all is well with my soul.
   No other name compares to the name of God,
   this thing I know.

98 Your light broke through my night

This is how we overcome

Words and Music: Reuben Morgan

1. Your light broke through my night, re-stored ex-cee-ding joy.
2. Your hand lif-ted me up, I stand on high-er ground.

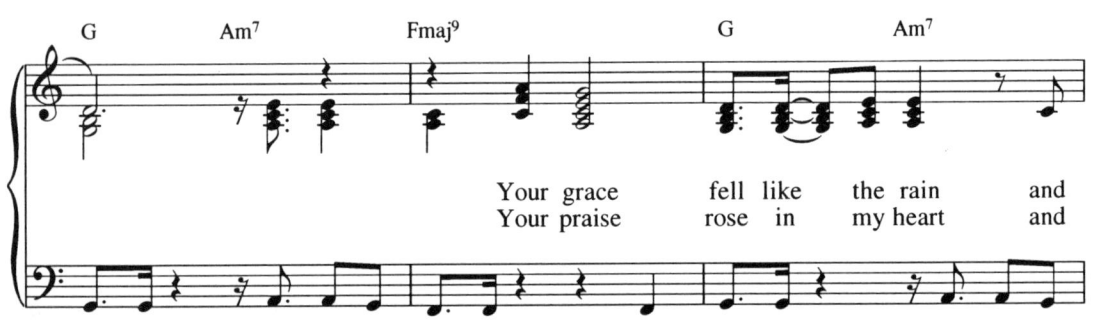

Your grace fell like the rain and
Your praise rose in my heart and

made this de-sert live.
made this val-ley sing. You have turned

my mourn-ing in-to danc-ing, You have

© Copyright 1998 Reuben Morgan/Hillsongs Publishing. Administered by Kingsway's Thankyou Music, P.O. Box 75, Eastbourne, East Sussex BN23 6NW, UK. Used by permission.

99 You said

Words and Music: Reuben Morgan

1. You said 'Ask and you will receive whatever you need.' You said 'Pray, and I'll hear from heaven and I'll heal your land.'

2. You said 'Your glory will fill the earth like wat'r o-ver sea.'

© Copyright 1998 Reuben Morgan/Hillsongs Publishing. Administered by Kingsway's Thankyou Music, P.O. Box 75, Eastbourne, East Sussex BN23 6NW, UK. Used by permission.

100 You've called me to worship
Jesus, you're everything
Words and Music: Mick Dalton

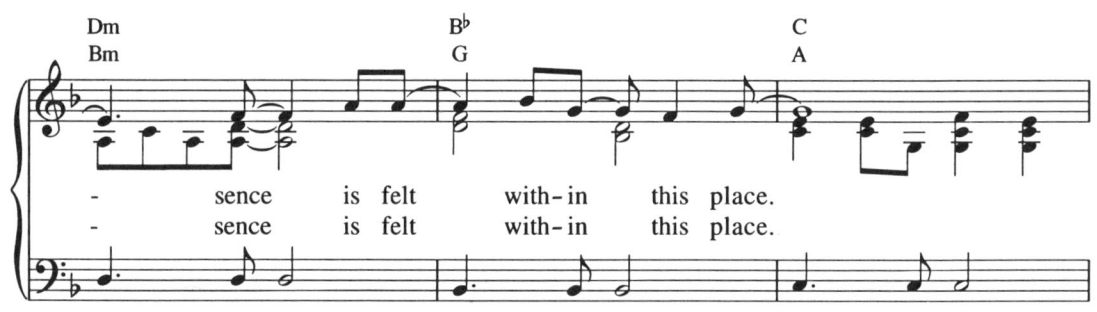
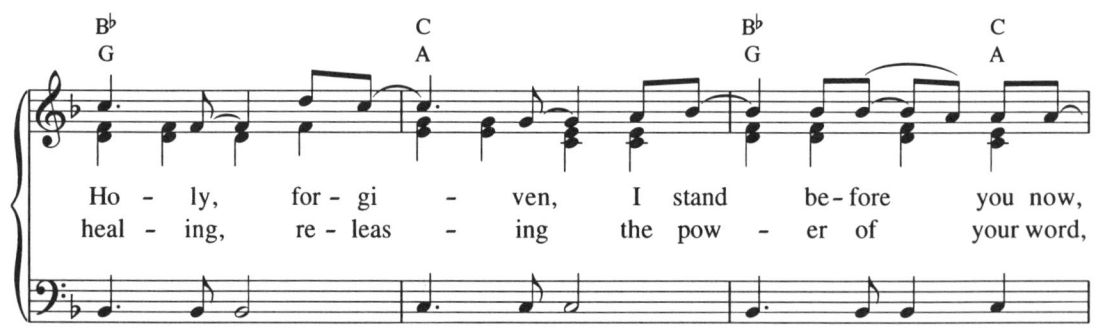

© Copyright 2000 Kevin Mayhew Ltd.

Index of First Lines, Titles and Recordings

This index gives the first line of each song. If a song is known by an alternative title, this is also given, but indented and in italics. A key to the recordings will be found at the end of this index.

	No	Rec		No	Rec
A heart of love	1	7	Heaven above and earth below	21	7
Ah, Jesus, Jesus	2	13	Here I am waiting	22	5
All creation bows	3	12	Here in your presence	23	22
All honour, all glory	4	24	Here I stand	24	12
All I know	5	1	Holy, holy, holy	25	15
All is well	97	10	Holy Spirit, I surrender	26	12
All that is within me, Lord	6	5	Holy Spirit, rain down	27	2
Anoint my hands for battle	7	14	I am not the same	28	5
A rising generation	8	5	I believe	29	23
As I come to you	9	8	I can feel	30	16
As we lift our hands to worship you	10	7	I can feel the Spirit of God is moving	31	21
Beautiful Lord, wonderful Saviour	11	2	I can hear heaven calling	32	23
Beautiful Saviour	12	7	I can see the day	33	1
Breathe on me	13	4	*I ever will proclaim*	36	16
By your side	71	5	*I feel like I'm falling*	75	5
Child of grace	26	12	I know he rescued my soul	34	5
Come, let's lift our praise	14	7	I lift up my eyes to your throne	35	3
Creation stands in awe	15	7	I lift your name	36	16
Deeper	32	23	I'll walk closer now	37	4
Deeper and deeper	16	7	*I'm here to worship you*	73	20
Dwelling-places	67	5	I'm lost for words to say	38	12
Eagles' wings	22	5	I'm set aside to worship you	39	12
Forever and always	17	7	I need your love	40	3
Forever loved by you	17	7	*In freedom*	8	5
Forgiven	38	12	*In Jesus' crown*	62	7
For such a time as this	44	22	In my life proclaim your glory	41	6
Freedom and liberty	18		*In you*	42	12
Free to dance	84	5	In you I've found my weakness	42	12
Glorified	93	2	*In your likeness*	54	22
God Almighty, let your presence	19	21	*In your presence*	63	9
God is so good	47	21	I open my life to you	43	3
God says 'Yes'	20	2	I see a southern land	44	22
Grace abounds to all	21	7	I see the Lord	45	26
Grace and mercy	94	15	It is he	46	3
Grateful, faithful heart	48	1	I've come to this house to celebrate	47	21
Great in power	74	5	I've found the power to be free	48	1
Have your way	85	3	I've got joy	49	19
Hear our praises	68	4	I walk by faith	50	25
Heart of Love	1	7	I was on your mind	51	8
Heaven	40	3	I will sing of your faithfulness	52	19

Title	No	Rec
I will worship	53	7
Jesus, Holy One of God	55	21
Jesus, I adore you	43	3
Jesus, I need you	54	22
Jesus, Jesus you are the one	55	21
Jesus, no one loves me more	56	17
Jesus, you're everything	100	10
Kingdoms will come	57	17
Let it be known	57	17
Let there be joy	58	15
Let the weak say I am strong	59	5
Let your glory fall	19	21
Let your glory	60	17
Let your Spirit come	61	19
Lifted up in our hopelessness	62	7
Lift our praise	14	7
Light to blinded eyes	69	7
Lord of all mercy	41	6
Lord of creation	63	9
Lord, to serve you is my joy	64	3
Lord, you are my solid ground	65	10
Lord, you are the one	66	19
Lovely are your dwelling-places	67	5
Make a way	77	21
May our homes be filled with dancing	68	4
Mercy	78	7
My heart will trust	37	4
My Redeemer lives	34	5
Never to be alone	69	7
No higher place	70	7
No name like Jesus	56	17
No other name	79	23
O dear God	71	5
O God of my comfort	72	7
O Lord, you're amazing	73	20
One in spirit	9	8
On your mind	51	8
Pour on your power	31	21
Praise him, you heavens	74	5
River	35	3
Sing of your great love	6	5
So let us rise to worship	10	7
Sound of a warrior	83	14
Standing tall in this wide space	75	5
Stay	28	5
Surely goodness	76	23
That's what we came here for	86	2
The only one	95	11
The Potter's hand	11	2
There is a sound of great rejoicing	77	21
There is hope beyond	78	7
There is no other name	79	23
There's a party goin' on	80	13
The Spirit of the Lord	81	13
The steadfast love of the Lord	82	3
The word is out	3	12
This is how we overcome	98	5
This is the day	52	19
This is the sound of a warrior	83	14
This song in my heart	84	5
This yearning deep within me	85	3
To the glory of your name	33	1
Touch me with your love	92	12
Unspeakable joy	49	19
We come into your presence	86	2
We have a vision	87	24
Well, we've come to this house	88	18
We will never be the same	89	20
What the Lord has done in me	59	5
When I feel you near	90	18
When the darkness fills my senses	91	5
Within my heart	92	12
Within your heart	39	12
Yes and Amen	20	2
Yet will I praise thee	66	19
You are a strong and firm foundation	93	2
You are high and lifted up	94	13
You are so faithful	95	11
You arrested me	65	10
You gave me a love	96	2
You're the light of my world	97	10
Your glory	88	18
Your light broke through my night	98	5
Your name is so beautiful	2	13
Your unfailing love	91	5
You said	99	5
You shine	64	3
You've called me to worship	100	11

Key to Recordings

#	Title	Label
1	Hillsong Update 19	Hillsong Music Australia / Hillsong Europe
2	Touching Heaven Changing Earth	Word
3	Simply Worship 3	Word
4	Shout To The Lord 2000	Integrity
5	By Your Side	Word
6	Unfailing Love	Kingsway
7	Deeper & Deeper	world wide worship ltd.
8	world wide worship 1	world wide worship ltd.
9	world wide worship 2	world wide worship ltd.
10	RiverSong Update 3	RiverSong
11	RiverSong Update 4	RiverSong
12	Beat Of The Heart	RiverSong
13	Souls For The Kingdom	Arrowhead Ministries UK
14	Sound Of A Warrior	Arrowhead Ministries UK
15	Grace And Mercy	Arrowhead Ministries UK
16	I Can Feel	Sounds of Paradise
17	Let It Be Known	Sounds of Paradise
18	What Jesus Means To Me	Sounds of Paradise
19	Unspeakable Joy	Sounds of Paradise
20	Worship In Action	SMART Productions
21	Make A Way	SMART Productions
22	Our Future	Lakes Music Australia
23	I Believe	Lakes Music Australia
24	Stand	Seam of Gold
25	War	Seam of Gold
26	Now	Seam of Gold

The recordings listed below are available from the following sources:

Hillsongs Update 19

Available direct from:
HILLSONG MUSIC AUSTRALIA
PO Box 1195
Castle Hill
NSW 1765
Australia

Tel: 00 612 8853 5300
Fax: 00 612 9680 3798
Email: hillsongs@hillsclc.org.au
Web: www.hillsongmusic.com.au

Or from:
HILLSONG EUROPE
23 Grove Road
Harpenden
Hertfordshire
AL5 1QG
United Kingdom

Tel: 01582 769184
Fax: 01582 767828
Email: h.beretta@virgin.net

Touching Heaven Changing Earth
Simply Worship 3
By Your Side

Available from your local Christian bookshop,
or direct from:
WORD MUSIC
9 Holdom Avenue
Bletchley
Milton Keynes
Buckinghamshire
MK1 1QR
United Kingdom

Tel: 01908 648440
Fax: 01908 648592
Email: premclub@wordonline.co.uk

Shout To The Lord 2000

Available from your local Christian bookshop,
or direct from:
INTEGRITY MUSIC EUROPE
PO Box 101
Eastbourne
East Sussex
BN21 4SZ
United Kingdom

Tel: 01323 430033
Fax: 01323 411981
Email: custcare@integrityeurope.com

Unfailing Love

Available from your local Christian bookshop,
or direct from:
KINGSWAY COMMUNICATIONS
PO Box 75
Eastbourne
East Sussex
BN23 6NW
United Kingdom

Tel: 01323 437700
Fax: 01323 411970
Email: gfoster@kingsway.co.uk

Deeper & Deeper
world wide worship 1
world wide worship 2

Available from your local Christian bookshop,
or direct from:
WORLD WIDE WORSHIP
Buxhall
Stowmarket
Suffolk
IP14 3BW
United Kingdom

Tel: 01449 737978
Fax: 01449 737834
Email: info@kevinmayhewltd.com

RiverSong Update 3
RiverSong Update 4
Beat Of The Heart

Available direct from:
RIVERSONG
PO Box 301
Windsor
NSW 2756
Australia

Tel: 00 612 4577 6555
Fax: 00 612 4577 6652
Email: riversong@zeta.org.au

Souls For The Kingdom
Sound Of A Warrior
Grace And Mercy

Available direct from:
ARROWHEAD MINISTRIES UK
40 Upper Lewes Road
Brighton
Sussex
BN2 3FH
United Kingdom

Tel: 01273 297809
Fax: 01273 297809
Email: arrowhead@zoom.co.uk

I Can Feel
Let It Be Known
What Jesus Means To Me
Unspeakable Joy

Available direct from:
SOUNDS OF PARADISE
2 Crowle Road
Paradise
SA 5075
Australia

Tel: 00 618 8336 3333
Fax: 00 618 8356 1744
Email: sop@senet.com.au

Worship In Action
Make A Way

Available direct from:
SMART PRODUCTIONS
PO Box 82
Victoria Park
WA 6100
Australia

Tel: 00 618 9362 5695
Fax: 00 618 9362 5695
Email: michael@cocperth.org.au

Our Future
I Believe

Available direct from:
LAKES MUSIC AUSTRALIA
PO Box 1038
Wangara
WA 6947
Australia

Tel: 00 618 9409 2021
Fax: 00 618 9409 2101
Email: neil@lakesclc.com

Stand
War
Now

Available direct from:
SEAM OF GOLD
Locked Bag 8
Dee Why
NSW 2099
Australia

Tel: 00 612 9975 6222
Fax: 00 612 9975 6223
Email: seamofgold@ccc.org.au

EFFECTIVE COMMUNICATION

JOHN CAPUTO
JO PALOSAARI
AND
KEN PICKERING

EDITED BY

JOHN NICHOLAS

DRAMATIC LINES, TWICKENHAM, ENGLAND
Effective Communication
text copyright © John Caputo Jo Palosaari and Ken Pickering 2003

No reproduction, copy or transmission
of any part of this publication may be
made without written permission of the
publisher.

Dramatic Lines
PO Box 201
Twickenham
TW2 5RQ
England

A CIP record for this book is
available from the British Library

ISBN 1 904557 13 9

Effective Communication
first published in 2003
by
Dramatic Lines
Twickenham England

Printed by The Dramatic Lines Press
Twickenham England

FOREWORD

This **EFFECTIVE COMMUNICATION Handbook** is one of a series primarily designed to support students and teachers preparing for examinations from the Drama and Speech syllabus of Trinity College, *London.*

However, the Dramatic Lines Handbooks have much wider applications. Not only do these books provide accessible and practical advice to students working towards ANY examination in Drama, Speech, Communication or Performing Arts, they also give invaluable help to those who wish to use their skills in a professional capacity as performers, teachers or communicators.

The Handbooks are quite literally something to keep to hand whenever you are working towards an important examination, performance, audition or presentation and you will find that they become your constant companions for a life in the Performance and Communications Arts.

Ken Pickering

Ken Pickering

Chief Examiner for Drama and Speech at Trinity College, *London* and Professor of Arts Education at the Institute for Arts in Therapy and Education

The authors gratefully acknowledge the help of Professor Harry Hazel of Gonzaga University USA in the preparation of this book.

CONTENTS

INTRODUCTION

1	Who is this book for?	1
2	How is the book structured?	1
3	How can this book be used?	4
4	What are the issues?	4

PART 1   THE TOOLS OF COMMUNICATION

	INTRODUCTION TO PART 1	9
5	Using PART 1	12
6	Native speakers of English communicating with non-native speakers	13
7	Non-native speakers of English	14
8	Teachers of non-native speakers of English	14
9	Native speakers and non-native speakers of English – great divide or wonderful opportunity?	15

LANGUAGE STRUCTURE

10	The communicative power of grammar	18
11	The role of grammar in fossilisation in non-native speakers	19
12	Useful grammar 'basics'	20
13	The English tense system	22
14	The use of modal verbs	28
15	The use of the active and passive	33
16	Expressing probability in conditional forms	36
17	Mixed conditionals	41

GRAMMAR CONSOLIDATION 1: TENSES

18	The English tense system – basic structures and functions	43

GRAMMAR CONSOLIDATION 2: FUTURES AND MODULES

19	Functional use of future tense constructions with modals	49

GRAMMAR CONSOLIDATION 3: PASSIVES

20 Use of the passive in the English language — 50

GRAMMAR CONSOLIDATION 4: CONDITIONALS

21 Summary of the conditional structures and functions — 52

WORDS

22 The power of words – choosing and using words carefully — 54
23 Using lexical sets — 55

SOUNDS

24 The communicative power of sounds — 66
25 Understanding at word level — 69
26 Understanding the emphasis – sentence stress — 71
27 Understanding the 'music' – intonation — 75

GLOSSARY — 79

PART 2 YOU AND YOUR VOICE

INTRODUCTION TO PART 2 — 85

HARNESSING NERVOUSNESS AND USING YOUR VOICE

28 Nervousness — 89
29 Physiological basis for speech-fright — 90
30 Psychological reasons for stress — 92
31 The good news about nervousness – the energizer effect — 93
32 Dealing with stage fright — 94
33 Managing the physical symptoms of stage fright — 95
34 Using your voice — 97
35 Projection — 97
36 Rate — 99
37 Vocal quality — 101
38 Inflection — 103
39 Articulation — 103
40 Putting together all the vocal elements — 105

PART 3   COMMUNICATION – CONTENT AND CONTEXT

INTRODUCTION TO PART 3 — 109

INTERPERSONAL COMMUNICATION

41	The experience of communication	113
42	Developing your communication potential and building your interpersonal style	115
43	What is interpersonal communication?	119
44	Culture	123
45	Ethical communication	126
46	Developing clear interpersonal ethics	127
47	Interpersonal goals	128
48	Gaining self-knowledge	129
49	Discovering commonality with others	130
50	Identifying the processes of communication	131
51	Applying communication principles	131
52	Recognising basic elements of communication	132
53	Striving for quality	133

ORATORY

54	The ability to talk effectively	136

MANAGING EFFECTIVE COMMUNICATION IN A VARIETY OF COMMUNICATION CONTEXTS

55	Preparing a speech for a known audience	148
56	Speaking to an unknown audience	154
57	Choosing a topic	154
58	Analysing your audience	156
59	Researching your topic	157
60	Putting your speech together	160
61	Remembering your speech	161
62	Using memory techniques	162
63	How the memory works – vivid imaging	163
64	Long-range preparation	166
65	Direct preparation	166
66	Rehearsing the speech	169
67	Humanistic and cross-cultural considerations – helping your audience to listen effectively	170

68	What listeners can do – understanding listening from the audience's perspective	173
69	Using the tools of communication effectively	176
70	In conclusion	180

NON-VERBAL FACTORS IN SPEECH DELIVERY

71	The elements of non-verbal communication	181
72	Dress	181
73	Posture	183
74	Gestures	184
75	Audio-visual aids	185
76	Types of visual aids	186

EVALUATING AND ASSESSING THE EFFECTIVENESS OF COMMUNICATION

77	Look to Shakespeare	189
78	The value of speech criticism	189
79	Evaluating a speech	190
80	Evaluating communication – a contextual approach	195

FORMS

Speech evaluation form	199
Persuasive speech evaluation form	201

INTRODUCTION

1 Who is this book for?

This book is intended for everyone who cares about good oral communication through the medium of the English language – anyone who wants to improve their own communication skills or the communication skills of others by extending their knowledge and deepening their understanding of the subject.

The book will be particularly useful to those who are preparing themselves or their students for some kind of assessment or examination in communication or public speaking. At the same time it will provide stimulating material for any reader who wishes to enrich the quality of their life and their relationships by becoming a better and more sensitive communicator.

The book is equally useful for those for whom English is their native language and for those who have acquired or are acquiring English as an additional language.

2 How is the book structured?

Like all aids to teaching and learning, this handbook needs to be used creatively and imaginatively. In order to do this you need to understand the way in which it is structured and you should spend a few moments studying the details of its structure and browsing through it to fix it in your mind.

PART 1   THE TOOLS OF COMMUNICATION

This deals with the tools of communication and contains sections on:

LANGUAGE STRUCTURE, GRAMMAR CONSOLIDATION, WORDS and SOUNDS.

PART 1 will be particularly helpful if you want to understand more about the way in which <u>spoken language</u> actually <u>works</u> and what is <u>unique</u> about <u>English</u>.

PART 1 also contains a glossary.

PART 2   YOU AND YOUR VOICE

This deals with the voice and the ways in which we can use it to ensure that our communication is both **effective** and **appropriate**.

PART 2 also refers you to other handbooks in this series that contain even more extensive consideration of voice and speech.

PART 3 COMMUNICATION – CONTENT AND CONTEXT

This examines the **content** and **context** of our communication and focuses on how we can best operate in inter-personal and public speaking situations.

PART 3 contains sections on:

INTERPERSONAL COMMUNICATION and ORATORY.

The **Preparation, Delivery** and **Assessment** of different kinds of speeches are examined in:

MANAGING EFFECTIVE COMMUNICATION IN A VARIETY OF COMMUNICATION CONTEXTS, NON-VERBAL FACTORS IN SPEECH DELIVERY and EVALUATING AND ASSESSING THE EFFECTIVENESS OF COMMUNICATION.

3 How can this book be used?

Now that you have a clear idea of the structure and contents of this handbook you will see that you can use it to suit your own needs. We are not assuming that you will necessarily want or need to work your way through each part. You may, for example, simply want to focus on the material on Public Speaking.

Each part begins with a short introduction explaining how it can best be used. There are activities for you to try out and responses for you to make, together with information on where you can go for additional help on a specific topic.

A most important point for you to grasp is that your approach should differ according to whether or not English is your or your students' native language and we have indicated clearly which topics are particularly aimed at non-native speakers.

Think of this handbook as a friend accompanying you on a journey and pause frequently to take breath and consider what has been said.

4 What are the issues?

The term 'communication' embraces a very wide

range of situations including the skills of public speaking, debating, discussing, listening, counselling, mediating, negotiating, teaching and marketing.

It involves addressing and interacting with audiences, clients, students, customers and colleagues in different situations such as 'live' meetings, telephone conversations and videoconferences.

<u>All the skills explored and developed in this handbook are relevant to communication contexts such as these.</u>

There is probably more 'talk' going on in the world now than at any time in history and the need for 'effective communication' is growing daily.

This is a skill that can be learned, developed and evaluated . . . . . and this handbook will help you in these exciting processes.

John S. Caputo, Jo Palosaari and Ken Pickering

PART 1
THE TOOLS OF COMMUNICATION

INTRODUCTION TO PART 1

Top athletes prepare for competitions by analysing and understanding the movement sequences of the sport. Because of this, every moment of their performance is maximised. A chef knows all about ingredients and cooking methods; how ingredients are blended, what works with what, and why. This understanding enables the chef to create wonderful food. An artist understands paints and perspectives, a dancer, movement and music, etc., etc.

In fact, any field in which an individual seeks to improve demands an understanding of the components involved.

Communication is no different. Effective spoken communication demands understanding of the elements of spoken communication, and how these elements can be manipulated to suit the communicative context:

- the type of communication

- the purpose of communication

- the style of communication

- the nature of the audience

- the potential range of feasible interaction patterns

Q Can you think of any other essential elements of spoken communication?

If your answer is yes, does it include language? Such an obvious element may seem unimportant – the fact that communication is taking place in a common language should be enough.

Q Or should it?

Whether the speakers and listeners are native speakers or non-native speakers of English, there are two major variables that play major roles in the quality of the communication:

➤ **The quality and nature of expression.**

➤ **The quality and nature of understanding.**

Within these two categories many factors are at play:

- use and understanding of grammar

- use and understanding of words

- use and understanding of voice

- use and understanding of affective psychological factors

PART 1 explores the tools of communication – what they are and how they work; and seeks to provide readers with a basic understanding of how **grammar, vocabulary** and **phonology** (sentence structure, words and sounds) work within spoken communication.

Readers with little or no previous knowledge of linguistics should gain useful insights into what makes spoken language powerful, and how their own use of language can become more effective.

Readers with linguistic knowledge may learn more about how to apply their theoretical knowledge to spoken communication practically and effectively.

Some common linguistic terminology is used, and all terms are shown in **bold**, explained briefly as they occur, and further defined in the accompanying glossary (see p.79).

NOTE: Readers should refer to the glossary for

full definitions of all the terminology used in PART 1.

Clarification is provided by consolidation tasks, which can be identified with the heading **Try this:**

Additional clarification is provided in the GRAMMAR CONSOLIDATION – which consists of practical, illustrative grammar summaries (starting on page 43 at the end of LANGUAGE STRUCTURE).

Readers are further guided to additional reference books concerned with theory and / or practical communication activities by the helping hand.

5 Using PART 1

All readers should read the introduction to gain an overview of the effect of language and psychology on communication.

When considering how to empower their communication, native speakers of English communicating with other native speakers may find the following topics useful:

- LANGUAGE STRUCTURE (see p.18)

    o   the use of **modal verbs**

    o   the use of the **active** and **passive**

- WORDS (see p.54)

    o   using **lexical sets**

- SOUNDS (see p.66)

    o   using **sentence stress**

    o   using **intonation**

6 Native speakers of English communicating with non-native speakers

In order to understand the potential for misunderstanding and avoid it wherever possible, native speakers of English communicating with non-native speakers should:

- read each topic

- complete the consolidation tasks

7 Non-native speakers of English

Non-native speakers of English should:

- read each topic

- complete the consolidation tasks – referring to the illustrative grammar consolidation summaries (see pages 43, 49, 50 and 52)

- seek further clarification where necessary from the suggested 'help' references

8 Teachers of non-native speakers of English

To help their students consolidate their understanding of affective factors, teachers of non-native speakers of English should:

- read each topic

- complete the consolidation tasks – use or adapt the illustrative grammar consolidation summaries (see pages 43, 49, 50 and 52)

- use the **helping hand** ✊ – additional resources can be useful in the classroom

9 Native speakers and non-native speakers of English – the great divide or a wonderful opportunity

Since the English language has increasingly become the lingua franca of international politics, business, entertainment and electronic communication, it has correspondingly become an incredibly rich resource for its native speakers.

The provision of English language courses and associated services is regularly in the top ten of Britain's invisible exports, and whole sectors of the tourism and publishing industries support it.

Britain is not the only country to benefit from this extended boom; thriving English Language Teaching (ELT) industries are growing in English speaking countries such as the U.S.A., Ireland, Canada, Australia and New Zealand, and even non-English speaking countries like China, Japan and Spain are rapidly expanding their internal markets.

It makes good sense then, when developing skills in effective communication, for native speakers and non-native speakers of English to understand both the restrictions and the opportunities that the difference in first languages (L1s) can mean to each participant in any cross-cultural communication process using

English as the common language.

Both native speakers and non-native speakers should seek to understand how the difference in their L1s affects each party's perception of oral communicative understanding, from two key perspectives:

➢ **What the speaker thinks s/he is saying.**

➢ **What the listener perceives the speaker is saying.**

Misunderstanding is possible even between speakers sharing and speaking in a common L1, and can occur for a number of reasons including psychological factors such as pre-knowledge, pre-conception and differences in individual goals.

When additional factors such as **the language structure (grammar), the words (lexis) and the sounds (phonology),** as well as cultural perceptions are added to the communicative equation, it is even more important for all participants to be aware of elements of spoken communication in order to avoid unnecessary misunderstanding, and to appreciate the ways it can be manipulated in order to increase the effectiveness of the message.

A good oral communicator is someone in control of the language; someone who can accurately understand what is being communicated to them, communicate her / his own message clearly, and play an active and guiding role in the development of the communicative event.

The topics: LANGUAGE STRUCTURE, WORDS and SOUNDS – are intended to be useful for both native and non-native speakers of English who are not linguists, but who will benefit from lay explanations of key issues in linguistics that may serve to increase communicative effectiveness, or alternatively may add to confusion and misunderstanding.

Do remember that basic terminology is used to enable interested readers to research the topics further using a more linguistic focus – explained in the glossary accompanying PART 1 (see p.79).

 Suggestions for further reading are provided in each section.

LANGUAGE STRUCTURE

10 The communicative power of grammar

A skilled communicator is a person who knows how to manipulate language in order to get the message across in the most effective way. In order to manipulate language successfully, the communicator must be able to use the **grammar** of the language efficiently.

It would be fair to say that at least half the message in any form of communication, be it spoken or written, is communicated through the way the language is being structured. Even an ungrammatical utterance, such as is heard in everyday speech, communicates an additional message – the lack of 'correct' **grammar** communicates the informality of the event, and perhaps indicates the regional setting, and whether the speaker is a native speaker or a non-native speaker.

Every language has its own **grammar system**, and languages are often compared on the basis of differences between these systems. Native speakers of English, while not needing to analyse the differences between English and other languages in order to communicate to non-native speakers, should be aware of some of the **grammar structures** that can be powerful tools if used thoughtfully, and similarly can then become fundamental sources of misunderstanding for non-native speakers.

Both native and non-native speakers should be aware of how, as listeners, they can be susceptible to the manipulation of language that occurs when **grammar** is used deliberately. Conversely, they should seek to maximise the ways in which they can make their messages more powerful by giving consideration to the structural presentation of the message.

11 The role of grammar in 'fossilisation' in non-native speakers

Non-native speakers often become **fossilised** in their use and understanding of the second language – they cannot seem to improve their abilities in the second language no matter how much they continue to study and to practise. A common cry from these frustrated language learners is "I don't have enough words", but this is a misleading deduction.

Part of the answer can usually be found in enabling these non-native speakers of English to understand and use language **structure** more effectively and so communicate more effectively with the words they do know.

An additional benefit of enabling more efficient use of grammar is that by using a few simple techniques employing grammar as a key tool of understanding, the language learner is also able to understand and acquire new and unfamiliar words more easily, and, equally importantly, to retain them in active use.

12   Useful grammar 'basics'

This book is not attempting to provide a course in **communicative grammar**, or even to approach **grammar** from a linguistic perspective. What is useful in the context of effective communication is to look at a few basic areas of **English grammar** that are particularly powerful, and consciously seek to improve the ways in which we utilise these grammar **structures** in order to improve the effectiveness of our communication.

Before we begin, however, we need to clarify some basic terminology: **structure** and **function**.

The structure of a phrase, a clause or a sentence

is the way in which the words are put together – the building of the utterance. The function of a phrase, clause or sentence is the meaning it conveys in context, because of its structure.

A mistake many learners, and unfortunately some teachers have made is to study grammar as a series of **structures** without paying due attention to the inherent meanings – the **functions**.

This goes a long way to explaining one prime cause of language learning fossilisation: because these non-native speakers assume that by learning how to structure the language in 'correct', discrete blocks, they "know English grammar", they are thus less open to further development of their language skills. A little knowledge can be a very dangerous thing, because the lack of **functional** understanding is compounded by a false belief in communicative ability.

In order to maximise the effectiveness of our spoken use of English language, let us examine the power inherent in a number of key areas of English **grammar** by looking at the following **grammatical systems: the English tense system, active and passive constructions, modal verbs** and **conditionals.**

👉 For further reading and help in teaching, learning and understanding English grammar:

👉 **For grammar explanations**

Cobuild Series, *Collins Cobuild English Usage*, Harper Collins 1990

R Hughes, R Carter and M McCarthy, *Exploring Grammar in Context*, CUP 2000

M Swan, *Practical English Usage*, OUP 1998

👉 **For communication activities that use grammar as a basis**

Jill Hadfield, *Communication Games* (graded series), Nelson 1992

👉 **For activities to help learners understand the English tense system**

Nick Hall and John Shepheard, *The Anti-grammar Grammar Book*, Longman 1991

13 The English tense system

There are twelve different ways of expressing the time

and duration of any action or state in English. In order to ensure that listeners understand the exact time reference, speakers should ensure that they are making full and accurate use of the **tense system** when appropriate. Conversely, listeners should be aware of the importance of paying attention to the time reference being communicated.

Native speakers of English

Should be aware that other languages do not necessarily explain time and action using similar tense structures, and may have fewer tense structures and therefore express some English tense concepts in other ways.

Non-native speakers of English

Should be aware of the type and amount of information being communicated by each tense structure, and should not ignore these implications just because they cannot translate the structure directly.

Broadly, we allocate time into three main bands: past,

present and future. Within these bands we differentiate the duration of the action, and the time it occurs in relation to the speaker's own perspective. For convenience, we will refer to these twelve expressions of time and action as tenses[1].

For the purpose of increasing effectiveness in communication in the context of this book it is not necessary to examine every **tense**, or even any **tense** in great detail, but it is worth considering the following:

1   The use of a **'simple' tense**, in which the verb is expressed in its basic form or with the addition of 'ed' (or similar if irregular, e.g. run / ran / run) implies a short, completed action or a permanent state.

    *EXAMPLE: Rob **ran** the marathon yesterday.*

What is important here is that the action took place yesterday, not its duration.

2   The use of a **'continuous' tense**, in which the verb is an auxiliary ending in 'ing', implies an

---

[1] A comprehensive summary of the twelve tense structures and their main functions is provided in Grammar Consolidation 1 p.43.

action carried out over a period of time.

*EXAMPLE: Rob **was running** for just over three hours.*

What is important here is how long the action took.

3. The use of a **'perfect' tense**, in which the auxiliary verb 'have' is used relates the action to another time or action.

*EXAMPLE: Rob **has run** marathons before, so the distance was no problem for him.*

What is important here is the fact that the action has been performed more than once, and so has an effect on the most recent action.

4. In English we have a system for chronological ordering of the past – the **'past perfect' tenses**. Within one sentence the order in which events took place can be communicated.

*EXAMPLE: Rob **had bought** new running shoes before he **heard** if he would be running in the London marathon.*

What is important here is the order of the three actions.

EXAMPLE: Rob **had been training** for three months before he **received** his confirmation through the post, so he was relieved when he opened the envelope.

What is important here is length of time the first action took.

5   In English we can chronologically order the future, and by so doing can imply a greater sense of determination.

Politicians are one breed of communicators who are fond of **'future perfect' structures** because using them can suggest positive and definite future action. By assuring completion of a task as yet not begun, politicians seek to instil more faith in their supporters of their ability to keep their promises during election campaigns.

EXAMPLE: We **will have transformed** the transport system before the end of our next term in office.

What is important here is the promised completion of a mammoth task before a known future milestone.

Continuing future commitment can also be implied.

EXAMPLE: By the time of the next election **we will have been improving** the health service for more than three years, and we won't stop there . . . . .

What is important here is the commitment of time already given, implying that there is no doubt about future continuation.

Native speakers of English

Should be aware that other languages do not necessarily have equivalent future tense structures, and may have fewer ways of explaining future time, duration and nature of the action, and probability within the one phrase in the way that these issues can be communicated in English. An understanding of the limit to the range of complex future structures or functions that the non-native speaking listener can understand is useful in cross-cultural communication.

⇨ Try this:

Imagine yourself in a situation in which you need to

make five important points persuasively. This might be a job interview, a presentation to colleagues, etc. At least one point should refer to the past, one to the present and one to the future.

i   Write your five points down as key words.

ii   Think about the **tense structures** you could use to make each point as firmly and succinctly as possible (you may wish to refer to GRAMMAR CONSOLIDATION 1 p. 43), trying to avoid the easy options of **past, present and future simple tenses.**

In that communicative situation, these five key sentences could form the basis and structure of your argument, and this small amount of preparation could ensure that these key points were spoken with confidence and assurance, and were noted and trusted by your listeners.

14   The use of modal verbs

Modal verbs are incredibly powerful words; they enable the communicator to express an opinion about likelihood or obligation in a single word, and, in combination with future **tense structures**, they enable these opinions to be expressed across a range of **functions.**[2]

When talking about the future, a speaker is usually either planning or predicting, since the action in question has not yet taken place. The **modal verb** that the speaker chooses is a clear indication of his / her opinion about future probability. Similarly, when using **future tense structures** incorporating **modal verbs** to speculate, assume or make a deduction, the speaker chooses the **modal verb** that expresses his / her degree of certainty.

⇨ **Try these:**

Where possible, do these activities with a partner and compare your opinions, and therefore your choice of modal verbs.

1   Match the percentage estimates of likelihood to these four predictions. (Remember, you are not matching your opinions on each issue, but rather the opinion of the communicator):

   0 %   30 %   70%   100%

---

[2] A comprehensive summary of the functional use of modal verbs tense constructions is provided in Grammar Consolidation 2 p.49.

- *The transport system **won't** have improved very much before the next election.*

- *Many voters **might** be considering a change of Government at the next election.*

- *The further education sector **may** be training more graduates in vocational occupations when pay rates improve.*

- *The threat to world order **will** continue to grow unless there is a more equitable distribution of wealth.*

2   You wish to persuade a colleague recovering from a heart attack to take better care of his health. Fill each gap with the *modal verb* that best reflects whether you are telling him what he is obliged to do, what you advise him to do, what you suggest would be beneficial, and what should be avoided at all costs.

must   should   could   shouldn't   mustn't

You _____ stop smoking.

You _____ eat too much fatty food.

You _____ take up some form of regular exercise.

You _____ join a gym.

3. Make your own deductions about these world-famous mysteries.

   must   may   might

Jack the Ripper _____ have been a member of the aristocracy.

Lee Harvey Oswald _____ have shot John F. Kennedy.

The FBI _____ have been responsible for Marilyn Monroe's death.

Native speakers of English

Should be aware that other languages do not necessarily have equivalents of English modal

verbs, and / or may express probability in different ways.

Non-native speakers of English

May never have clarified the difference in meaning that each modal verb implies and so may fail to understand the significance of probability or obligation in context.

In spoken English the effect of stress patterns (see SOUNDS p.66) may cause the modal verb to be 'swallowed' and therefore difficult for the non-native speaking listener to hear. It is wise to emphasise the modal verb when you want to communicate your opinion about probability clearly.

Many non-native speaking listeners confess to 'ignoring' the modal verbs when they are listening to English speakers, so it is often useful to reiterate a strongly held opinion about likelihood (to reformulate the opinion) when it is important that this part of the message be clearly understood.

15 The use of the active and the passive

Passive constructions have undoubtedly saved many a communicator a great deal of money over the years in libel suits that didn't make it to court. Beloved by political commentators, journalists and scandalmongers, rued by libel lawyers, the **passive** is one the English language's most manipulative tools.

By using a **passive construction** it is possible to imply, for example, another person's responsibility for a misdemeanour or mistake, without actually making a direct accusation. It is possible to remain deliberately vague about the source of a rumour, and it is also possible to issue directives while sounding unfailingly polite. Persuasive communicators keep their chosen focus uppermost in the listener's mind while not denying the role of the perpetrator.[3]

On any day, a selection of examples of the **passive** in use can provide us with interesting insights into the usefulness of **passive constructions**:

EXAMPLE: **Public reaction** to Camilla's appearance in the royal box **will be watched** carefully.

Private Eye

---

[3] A summary of the main functions of the passive, shown in the range of tense structures commonly used with the passive, is provided in Grammar Consolidation 3 p.50.

Who **exactly** will be watching? The orchestrators of royal, political or celebrity appearances are rarely revealed, but their roles are often highlighted in faintly sinister overtones that the passive construction can provide.

EXAMPLE: I don't think **Will has been treated** *like a winner.*

(Dec, an entertainer – quoted in Heat magazine)

By whom **exactly**? This celebrity is wisely choosing not to make his accusation directly; after all, he may be the next victim.

While the passive is a structure that is often used, with some degree of consideration, in written communications, it can be very effectively used in spoken communication:

➪ Try these:

1   Match the communicative purposes on the left with the sentences on the right:

i	*Give advice without causing offence*	**a**	**It has been said that he'll leave the company after the next AGM.**

ii	Suggest that an opinion is a commonly held belief	**b**	**The programme has been decided and no changes can be made at this stage.**
iii	Spread a rumour with a degree of anonymity	**c**	**It is generally believed that most people consult lifestyle managers regularly.**
iv	Non-aggressive self-promotion	**d**	**The information must have been leaked by someone very close to the PM.**
v	Make a point politely but forcefully.	**e**	**Reports are usually prepared on a monthly basis in this department.**
vi	Make an indirect accusation	**f**	**I was regarded as a key member of the team at the last conference event.**

2 Think about at least three important situations where you could use the **passive construction** to increase the effectiveness of

your communication of a key point.

Q What would you say in each situation?

Native speakers of English should be aware that other languages do not necessarily construct a 'passive concept' in the same way that the English language does.

Similarly, passive constructions may be used for other functions.

Non-native speakers may never have clarified for themselves the passive construction and range of possible functions in English.

When using passives in spoken communications with non-native speakers, English speakers should utilise sentence stress and intonation fully (see SOUNDS).

16 Expressing probability in conditional forms

English has a wonderfully logical system for expressing probability based on the current situation – a set of four structures which are normally known as

conditionals [4].

The **conditionals** are sentences made of two distinct clauses – the **condition clause** and the **outcome clause** – and are identified as numbers 0, 1, 2 and 3. The logic is that as the numbers identifying each **conditional** increase so does the degree of probability, and an increasing 'distance' between the tense, or time expressed, in each clause represents these changes structurally.

Judicious use of **conditional structures** can add particular emphasis and clarity to all forms of spoken communication.

⇨ **Try these:**

1   Experiment with **conditionals** using the topic of environmental issues.

    Add emphasis to a fact or truism by using the **0 conditional:**

---

[4] A summary of the main functions of the four conditional structures, giving illustrative examples, is provided in Grammar Consolidation 4 p.52.

*"Every time we **pump** more waste into our sea, we **kill** more fish."*

Using the **present tense** in each **clause**, think of two more key facts about man's treatment of the environment.

2   Express your opinion about the future by using the **1 conditional**.
(Note the use of **modal verbs** in the **outcome clause**)

*"If the USA **does not honour** the Kyoto treaty, a new international agreement **must be reached**."*

*"If the developing world **does not receive** more funding, poorer countries **will not be able** to reduce their greenhouse gas emissions."*

*"If a new fishing policy **is not agreed**, the European fishing industries **may suffer** even greater hardship."*

Using the **present tense** in the **condition clause** and the **future tense** in the **outcome clause**, make three predictions of your own about the future of our environment based on current environmental practice. Try to use a different **modal verb** in each sentence.

3   Express hopes and wishes about the future of our environment using the **2 conditional.**
(Note that the **condition clause** states the opposite of fact, and also note the use of **modal verbs** in the **outcome clause**)

*"If I **were** on the council, I **would introduce** an efficient household recycling system."*

*"If the government really **wanted** to reduce greenhouse gas emissions, they **could increase** taxes on car use in all cities, and improve public transport."*

*"If world governments **agreed** to fund green industry in developing countries, the level of pollution **would be reduced** significantly."*

Using the **past tense** in the **condition clause** and the **future tense** in the **outcome clause**, express three of your own wishes for future environmental policy making. Try to use a different **modal verb** in each sentence.

4   Express the impossible in order to add emphasis to a theme using the **3 conditional**.

(Note that the **condition clause** states the opposite of what has already happened, and the **outcome clause** suggests what could have happened in different circumstances)

*"If man **had used** science and technology more wisely, the world **might have become** a cleaner place to live in."*

*"If such large amounts of effluent **hadn't been pumped** into the North Sea, many fishermen **wouldn't have lost** their livelihoods."*

*"If we **had put** more money into alternative fuels, we **wouldn't have become** so dependent on oil and the oil-rich states."*

Using the **past perfect tense** in the **condition clause** and the **future perfect tense** in the **outcome clause**, express three of your own wishes for future environmental policy making. Try to use a different **modal verb** in each sentence.

17 Mixed conditionals

The English language is wonderfully flexible, and this is demonstrated most often in spoken English.

*EXAMPLE: "If we **hadn't had** an industrial revolution, the world **would be** a different place today."*

Mixing the impossibility of the **condition clause** in the **3 conditional** with the suggestion of greater likelihood in the **outcome clause** adds an emphasis of inevitable truth.

⇨ **Try this:**

Now that you have considered the four basic forms of **conditionals**, listen and look out for examples of **mixed conditionals** i.e. structures that use the **conditional** form of a **condition clause** and an **outcome clause** – but that don't follow the 'rules' for **tense structure**. Collect three authentic examples and think about how the 'mixing' affects the speaker's meaning in each case.

Native speakers of English

Should be aware that other languages do not necessarily construct conditionals in the same way that the English language does, or express the same range of conditional possibilities within

41

one-sentence utterances.

Non-native speakers of English

May never have clarified for themselves the range of possibilities in English conditionals, or consolidated their functional understanding of the range of structures used. Mixed conditionals add even more possibilities for confusion and misunderstanding.

When English speakers are using conditionals in spoken communications with non-native speakers, they should consider the potential for misunderstanding, reformulate or concept check where necessary, and utilise stress patterns and intonation fully (see SOUNDS p.66).

GRAMMAR CONSOLIDATION 1: TENSES

18 The English tense system – basic structures and functions

PRESENT SIMPLE: *an habitual action*

Structure

S   V1
I usually see some friends every week.

```
           X   X   X   |   X   X   X
Timeline  Past           Now           Future
```

a fact or belief

Structure

S V1
Britain is an island and the people have an 'island mentality'.

```
Timeline  Past           Now           Future
```

PRESENT CONTINUOUS: *an action happening now*

Structure

       to be   ...ing
       S   V1
At the moment Sarah is sitting at her desk, staring into space.

```
Timeline  Past           Now           Future
```

A definite near future plan

Structure

to be   ...ing
S V1
I am going home at 5 o'clock on the dot today.

```
                          X
Timeline  Past           Now           Future
```

PAST SIMPLE: completed action at a definite past time

Structure

　　S　　　V2
Alison went to Spain last summer.

| Timeline | Past | X | Now | Future |

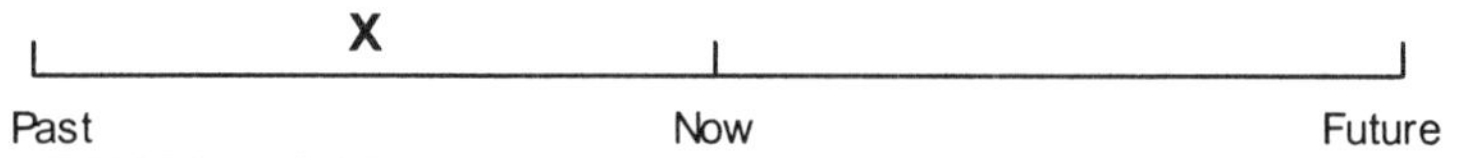

PAST CONTINUOUS: continuous completed past action over a time period

Structure

　　　to be　　　...ing
　S　V2
Terry was studying in Liverpool during 1990.

| Timeline | Past | Now | Future |

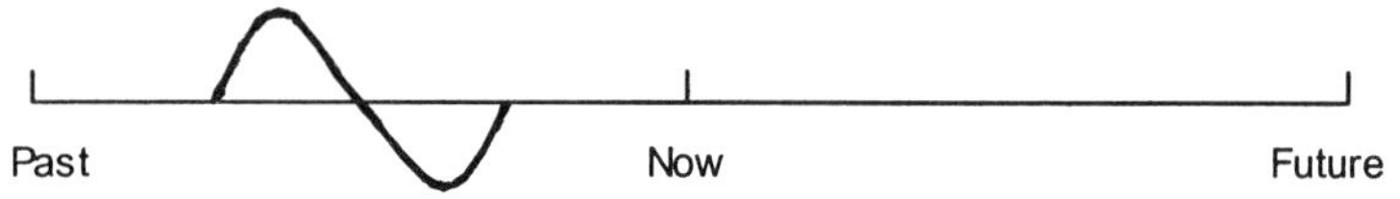

Two simultaneous past actions

Structure

　　to be　...ing
　S　V2
He was living at the University while he was studying.

| Timeline | Past | Now | Future |

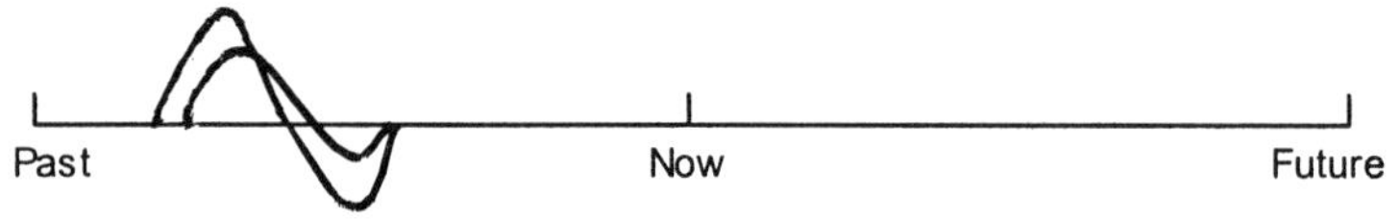

Continuous past action that is interrupted

Structure

　　　　　　　　　　　　　　　　　　　　　　　　　　　　　　　　to be
　S　　　　V2　　　　　　　　　　　　　　　　　　　　　　　　S　V2
The phone call came through to the department secretary while he was ...ing taking his maths exam.

| Timeline | Past | Now | Future |

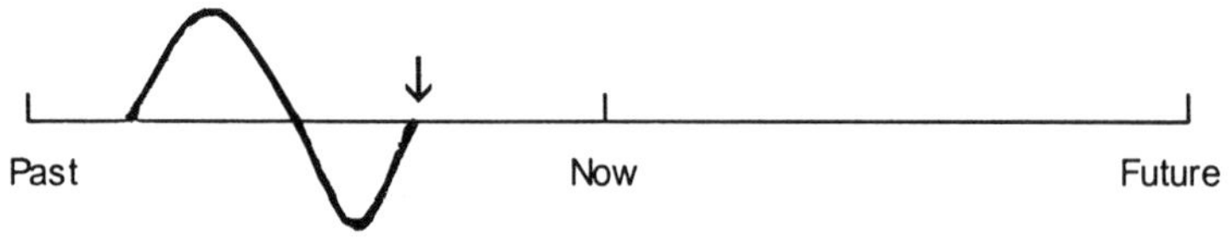

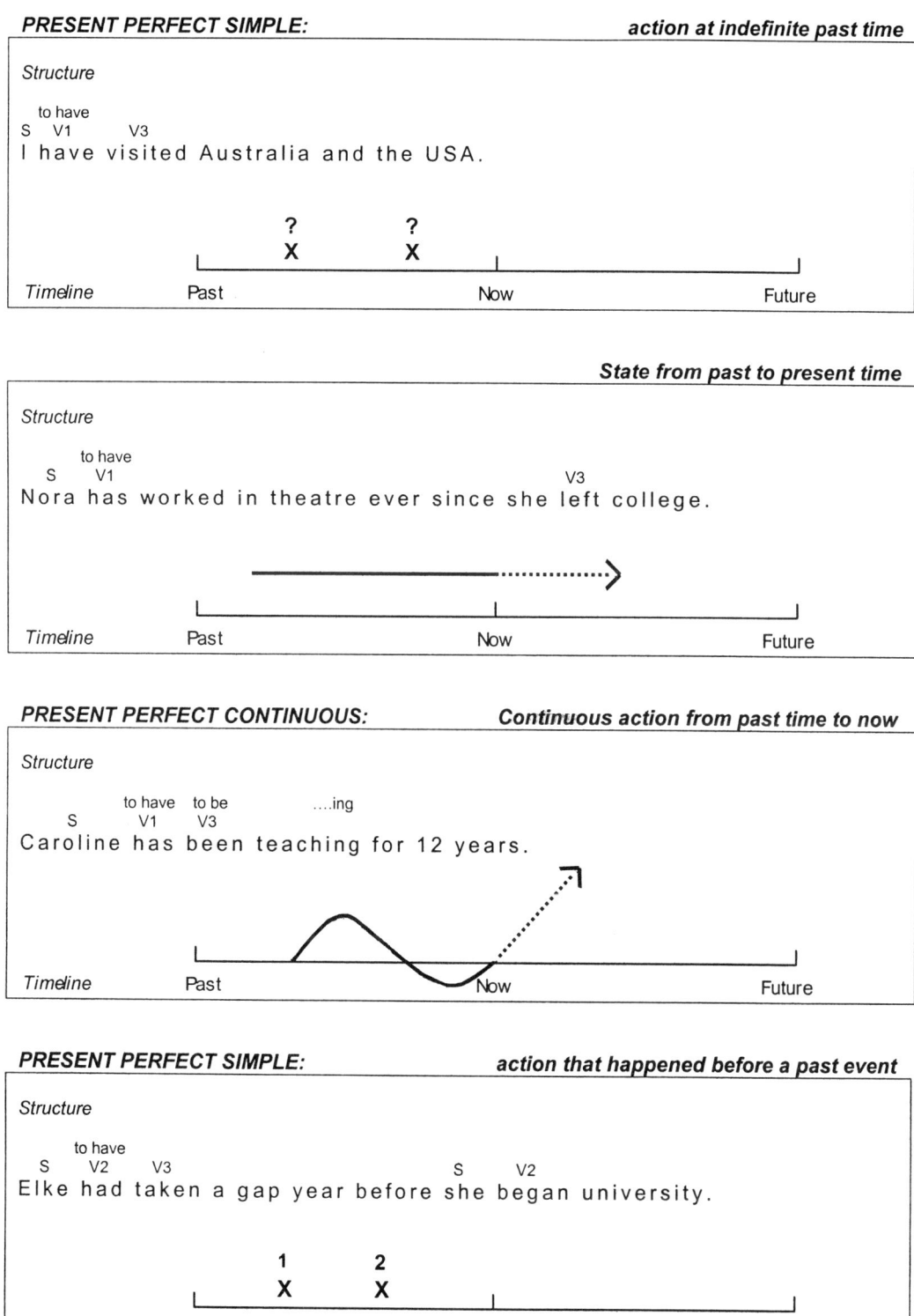

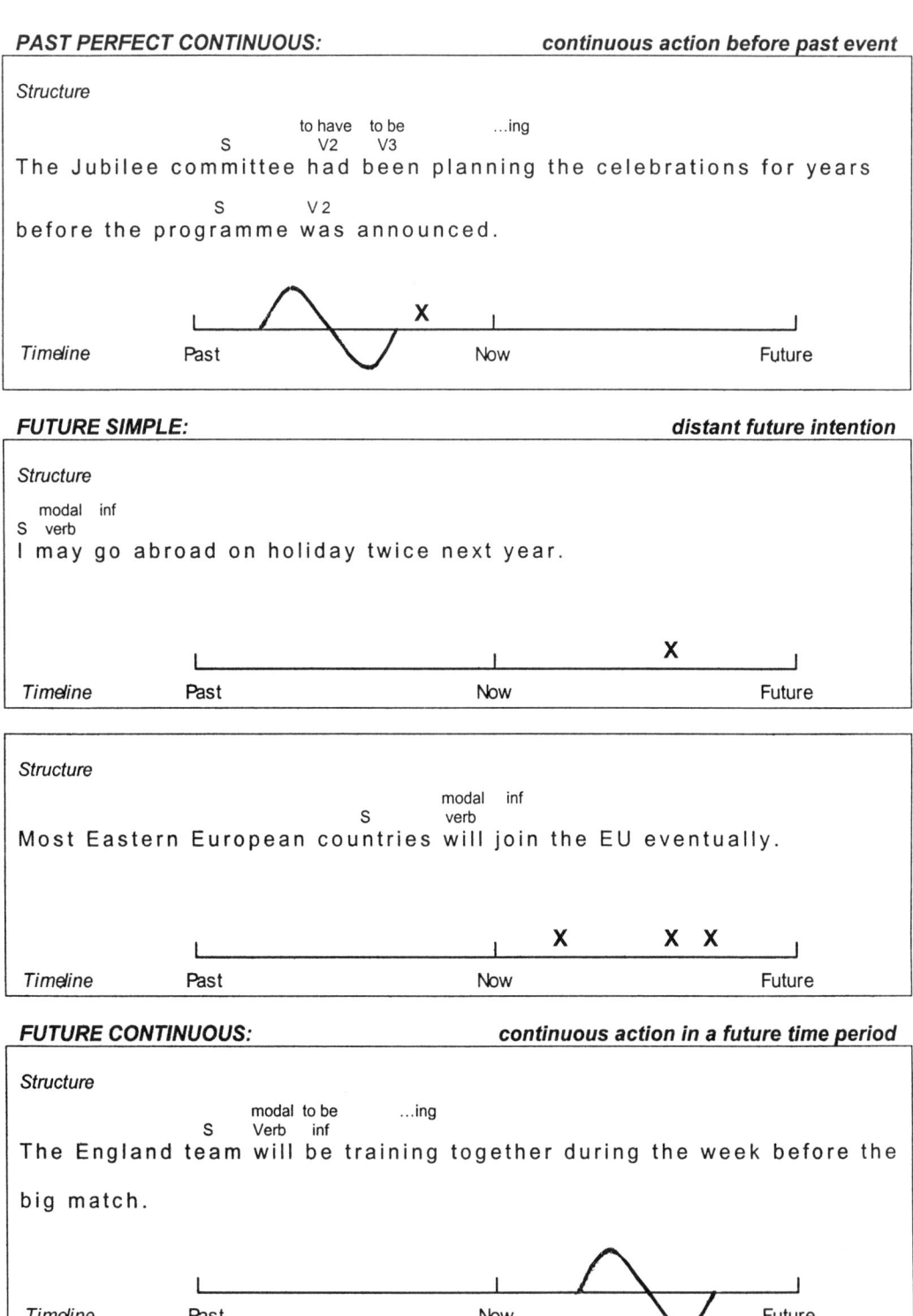

FUTURE PERFECT SIMPLE: *completed future action before future time*

Structure

```
           modal  to have
     S     verb   Inf
```
The Queen will have opened the new Arts Centre before the summer programme begins.

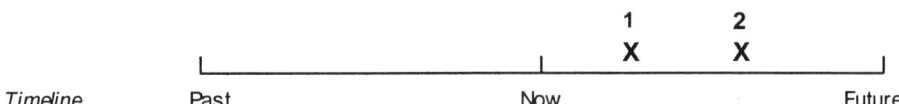

Timeline — Past — Now — Future

FUTURE PERFECT CONTINUOUS: *continuous action until future time*

Structure

```
             modal  to have  to be   ...ing
       S     verb   inf      inf
```
In the future, many more couples will have been living together for more than ten years before they marry.

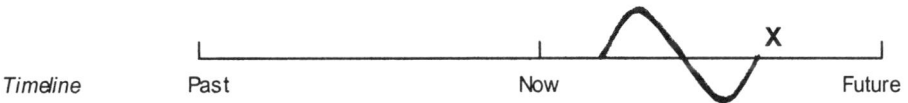

Timeline — Past — Now — Future

CODE:

S	Subject	∿	Continuous action
V1	Finite verb	—	State
V2	Past verb	X	Single action
V3	Past participle	1 X	First action
Inf	Infinitive		
?	Action at any unknown time	2 X	Second action
↓	Interruption	...ing	'ing form of verb

STRUCTURAL HINTS:

All *present* and *past simple tenses* use only one verb.

The *future simple tense* uses a modal verb + infinitive (- to).

All *present* and *past continuous tenses* use the verb 'to be' to define time and the 'ing form to describe the action.
The *future continuous tense* uses a modal verb + 'to be' infinitive (-to) + 'ing form to describe action.

All *present* and *past perfect tenses* use the verb 'to have' to define time + past participle.
The *future perfect tense* uses a modal verb + 'to have' infinitive (-to) + past participle.

All *present* and *past perfect continuous tenses* use the verb 'to have' to define time + 'to be' past participle + 'ing form to describe the action.
The *future perfect continuous tense* uses a modal verb + 'to have' infinitive (-to) + 'to be' past participle + 'ing form to describe action.

SUMMARY:

All future tenses need an auxiliary modal verb: *will / shall / must / may / should / ought to / might / could / can / would (conditional use)* + the action verb.
All continuous tenses need 'to be': *was / am, is, are* + the 'ing form.
All perfect tenses need 'to have': *had / have.*
All perfect continuous tenses need 'to have' + 'to be' past participle: *been* + 'ing form.

FUNCTIONAL HINTS:

All simple tenses refer to a single action or a state.
All continuous tenses refer to a period of time.
All perfect tenses relate one time to another.
All future tenses use the modal verb to express the degree of probability.

GRAMMAR CONSOLIDATION 2: FUTURES AND MODULES

19 Functional use of future tense constructions with modals

FUNCTION	DEGREE OF LIKELIHOOD (Probability)	FUTURE SIMPLE	FUTURE CONTINUOUS	FUTURE PERFECT SIMPLE	FUTURE PERFECT CONTINUOUS
ABILITY		can			
INTENTION	100% ↑ 50% ↓ 50%	will / shall may might	will / shall may might	will / shall may might	will / shall may might
PREDICTION	100% ↑ 50% ↓ 50%	will may might / could	will may might / could	will may might / could	will may might / could
OBLIGATION	100%	must			
ADVICE	↑ 50%	should / ought to	should / ought to		
SUGGESTION	↓ 50%	could	could		
ASSUMPTION	100% ↑ 50% ↓ 50%	must may might / could			
DEDUCTION	100% ↑ 50% ↓ 50%			must may might / could	must may might / could
1 Conditional INTENTION / LIKELY OUTCOME	100% ↑ 50% ↓ 50%	will may might	will may might		
2 Conditional WISH / DREAM UNLIKELY OUTCOME		would / could	would / could		
3 Conditional REFLECTION / REGRET				would could may might	would could may might

GRAMMAR CONSOLIDATION 3: PASSIVES

20 Use of the passive in the English language

TO ADD EMPHASIS WHEN SPEAKING

This song was composed by John Lennon, not Paul McCartney.

TO KEEP THE MAIN SUBJECT IN FOCUS

Before **the Queen** meets the Prime Minister **she will have been saluted** by the regiment.

WHEN THE AGENT OF THE ACTION IS UNKNOWN

The girl had been shot at the station before the last train arrived.

WHEN THE AGENT OF THE ACTION IS OBVIOUS OR UNIMPORTANT

This evening's edition is being printed at the moment.

WHEN THE AGENT OF THE ACTION IS NOT CLEARLY IDENTIFIABLE

Many cars were being destroyed while the police tried to control the rioters.

WHEN THE AGENT OF THE ACTION DOES NOT WANT TO BE IDENTIFIED

The Minister will be asked to resign within the next few days.

TO OFFER AN EXCUSE

I'm sorry; I can't come to the pub because **I've been asked** to work late.

TO GIVE ORDERS AND INSTRUCTIONS IN A POLITE AND IMPERSONAL WAY

Dogs are not permitted in the park but **can be exercised** on the common.

The *passive form* is constructed in the following way:

- 'the object' of the active form + the verb 'to be' which contains the tense + the past participle (3), which is the verb for the action
- the remaining part of the sentence contains the meaning of the tense

EXAMPLE:

'Macbeth' was written by Shakespeare in the sixteenth century
  subject   to be   V3   agent   function of the *past simple*

GRAMMAR CONSOLIDATION 4: CONDITIONALS

21 Summary of the conditional structures and functions

Conditional sentences are useful communication tools, for two reasons:

- ➤ **They add emphasis to the point you wish to make.**

- ➤ **They illustrate, or act as an example of your point of view.**

THE 0 CONDITIONAL

Describes a fact or belief – implies that the point cannot be disputed.

GRAMMATICAL STRUCTURE:

condition clause	outcome clause
If you drop an egg	it breaks.
PRESENT TENSE	**PRESENT TENSE**

EXAMPLE: *If a country is a member of the EU, it is bound by EU regulations.*

THE 1 CONDITIONAL

Describes the outcome of a possible future condition – illustrates your opinion about possibilities.

GRAMMATICAL STRUCTURE:

condition clause	outcome clause
If it is sunny tomorrow	the cricket match will go ahead.
PRESENT TENSE	**FUTURE TENSE**

EXAMPLE: *If new countries join the EU, some facets of the union may change.*

THE 2 CONDITIONAL

Describes the outcome of an unlikely future condition – can illustrate your wishes or dreams.

GRAMMATICAL STRUCTURE:

condition clause	outcome clause
If I were rich	*I would never work again.*
PAST TENSE	**FUTURE TENSE** (CONDITIONAL MODAL)

EXAMPLE: If all the EU countries agreed on every aspect of political and economic union, the union would be a united and powerful group of nations.

THE 3 CONDITIONAL

Describes the relationship between two past events – can be used to illustrate what DID happen and why, or what COULD have happened, but didn't.

GRAMMATICAL STRUCTURE:

condition clause	outcome clause
If I hadn't studied hard at school	*I wouldn't have been able to go to university.*
If I had stayed in my last job	*I would have become ill.*
PAST PERFECT TENSE	**FUTURE PERFECT** *TENSE*

EXAMPLE: If the UK hadn't joined the EU, a northern European union might have developed from greater association with the Scandinavian and Baltic countries.

WORDS

22 The power of words – choosing and using words carefully.

All languages share the concept of **synonyms** – using different words to express the same, or a very similar meaning. Skilled communicators know when and how to choose exactly the right word to express their exact meaning, in order to give greater clarity to what they are saying.

Because native speakers have been exposed to varied uses of English for most of their lives, they have the advantage of innate **lexical** knowledge. At the very least they will probably have a far greater passive understanding of a broader range of words, **phrasal verbs** and **collocations** than a non-native speaker – with the exception of a few with very advanced English language skills.

Native speakers of English

Should be aware that non-native speakers are not as likely to have as great a range of passive understanding as their active use of vocabulary might suggest.

While learning and using individual words may not

pose many problems for capable language learners, collocations, colloquialisms and phrasal verbs, are usually much more difficult to acquire.

It is possible, and certainly desirable, for both native and non-native speaking individuals to develop their active and effective use of English lexis.

 For more information about how vocabulary is learned:

R Carter and M McCarthy *Vocabulary and Language Teaching,* Longman 1988

R Gairns and S Redman *Working With Words*, CUP 1992

N O Schmidtt & M McCarthy *Vocabulary, Description, Acquisition and Pedagogy*, CUP 1997

23 Using lexical sets

➢ **Lexical sets** are groups of words bound by a common element.

➢ **Semantic sets** are bound by common elements of meaning.

EXAMPLE: house, cottage, flat, bungalow, tepee, etc. All these words identify dwellings.

> A **morphological set** is bound by a common **grammatical** function.

*EXAMPLE: red, dark, silent, sensible etc. are **adjectives**. They all describe the word they are referring to.*

Good conversationalists stimulate the minds of their companions with 'vividity' – vivid imagery; good public speakers carry their audiences with powerful word images.

Both native and non-native speakers can improve their communicative word power by developing the habit of considering their choice of words.

If **lexical** choices are actively considered when preparation time is available, the practice will stimulate the development of active use of a broader vocabulary. This, in turn, will assist the communicator to be more descriptive, more precise, more concise and therefore more interesting to listeners.

<u>Consider the power of the words you are using, and choose your words carefully.</u>

⇨ **Try these:**

1. Think of at least three words for each **lexical set**, as represented by the sketches. Consider both the **morphology** (grammatical function) and **semantics** (meaning) of your choices.

    i   NOUNS (names of things)

    ii ADJECTIVES (describing words)

iii VERBS (action words)

iv ADVERBS (describing how, where or when an action is being performed)

Q In each set, which do you feel is the most powerful word?

2   You want to sell your home. Describe it as persuasively as you can.

3   You are annoyed by the actions of a close associate. Tell your friend why you are so annoyed.

➪ Points to consider:

- **Communicators** must also be aware of the level of understanding and patience of their listeners.

➢ You should use more complex words sparingly, giving greater impact to the key points you wish to make, rather than showering your listeners with 'too many big words'.

➢ You should try to find the right balance between understanding and impact.

- **Adjectives** – while adjectives undoubtedly add 'colour' to speech, the use of too many may distract the listener from the point being made.

➢ One well-chosen **adjective**, spoken with added emphasis, will have far more impact than two or three indiscriminately chosen adjectives.

- ➢ A list of **adjectives** can become a central point in a speech - if used together with features of phonology (see SOUNDS p.66).

- ➢ **Single syllable adjectives**, spoken with equal emphasis, can alert listeners to strong opinion.

EXAMPLE: The <u>crude, base</u> behaviour of these people can only ...

- ➢ **Multi-syllable adjectives** can imply gravity.

EXAMPLE: His theory is <u>fundamentally</u> sound, and borne out by extensive research ...

- • **Alliteration** – used with **sentence stress** gains attention and adds emphasis.

EXAMPLE: A <u>short, sharp shock</u> is necessary to force ...

- • **Verbs** and **adverbs** – not every action needs to be described.

- ➢ A well-chosen **verb** can be also be descriptive.

➢ **Adverbs** should be used when the additional meaning they give is necessary and valuable.

EXAMPLE: The metropolitan police are struggling to cope with the sharp increase in violent crime, and younger criminals are <u>flagrantly</u> disregarding the threat of arrest.

- **Reporting verbs** – these words describe the way something is said, and are used both with **direct speech** and **indirect** (reported) **speech.**

Although **reporting verbs** are more commonly used for effect in written communication, they can be influential tools when suggesting the manner in which a third party has spoken, and can make speech succinct.

🡆 **Compare these four sentences:**

Direct speech
"I'll kill you," he <u>said</u> threateningly.
"I'll kill you," he <u>threatened</u>.

Indirect speech
He <u>said</u> that he would kill me.
He <u>threatened</u> to kill me.

- **Phrasal verbs** – for almost every commonly used **verb** there is an equivalent **phrasal verb** (a **verb** composed / made up from another **verb** and a **preposition**).

Phrasal verbs are much more difficult for non-native speakers to understand, partly because there are so many of them and partly because so many are so similar.

⇨ **Try these:**

1   Think of an equivalent **phrasal verb** for each **verb**:

Ignite   dress   compose   reduce   reprimand

Q   How many of these **verbs** could be represented by more than one **phrasal verb**, with each giving a different meaning to the original **verb**?

2   Time yourself.

Q   How many **phrasal verbs** can you think of in twenty seconds beginning with 'get'?

- **Idioms** – every language has its own **idioms**. It is important to remember that there may be differences in the way **idioms** are expressed from one language to another.

  > A communicator when speaking to non-native listeners should ensure that using **idioms** does not cause misunderstanding.

  > Non-native speakers should check that they are using the right **idioms** to express the meaning they wish to convey; their own **idioms** do not necessarily translate.

Try this:

Match the idioms from Finnish and English.

ENGLISH:

1 *Make a mountain out of a molehill.*
2 *It's like pulling teeth.*
3 *They're tarred with the same brush.*
4 *Take coals to Newcastle.*

FINNISH [1] *(direct translations):*

A It's like drinking tar.
B Make out of a fly an ox.
C Carry water to the well.
D They're the same land.

➪ And finally . . . . . try this:

Good story telling depends on the effective use of **vocabulary**.

i Think of a story from your life you wish to tell in as interesting a way as possible.

ii Note down the key elements and turning points of the story in chronological order.

iii Using these points as prompts, record yourself telling your story.

iv Play back the recording, and note each sentence in which you could have chosen your words more effectively.

---

[1] Key: 1 and B, 2 and A, 3 and D, 4 and C.

v   Record your story again and compare the two versions.

vi Think about any differences in the choice of words that you might make if you were telling this story to a non-native speaker.

 For more information on phrasal verbs:

Cobuild Series, *Collins Cobuild Dictionary of Phrasal Verbs,* Collins 1989

 For vocabulary learning activities:

Peter Watcyn-Jones & Deirdre Howard-Williams *Vocabulary Games and Activities*, Longman 2001

SOUNDS

24 The communicative power of sounds

It's interesting to see the way babies respond to the familiar voices of their parents, and even sometimes uncanny the way they seem to understand what is being said to them; when they are being spoken to lovingly, when they're being warned, or scolded.

While babies understand so much of what is said to them, they are still only in the process of acquiring their first language, and so are not yet familiar with a wide range of words or language structures. They do, however, understand the sound of the language, and the way certain words and phrases are repeated to them in the same tone of voice.

Animals also respond to the particular sound of a voice. Family pets, for example, know when they are being directed, given affection or disciplined, and working animals and farm animals come to recognise certain commands without actually understanding any language components.

Since it is the sound of the language that is provoking response, if we wish to understand why the communication is effective, we need to analyse what these receivers of spoken communication are actually responding to.

Q What are the elements of the sounds that are meaningful?

Q What is it about familiar sounds that gives them their identifiable characteristics?

For beings who don't (yet) use the English language but who understand small chunks of it, the way something is said is more understandable than what is actually being said.

➡ **Try this if you have a pet or young baby who knows you well. If possible, record your voice:**

i   Think of three or four common words or phrases that your baby or pet usually responds to, and say each of them at least once, using the tone of voice you normally attach to the word or phrase. Observe the response in your pet or child.

ii A little later, use each of these words or phrases again, but pitch your voice in an entirely different way; emphasise, or **stress** different syllables and / or words, make your voice rise ↗ where it would normally fall and fall ↘ where it would normally rise, speak softly where you would normally add extra sound, and add volume where your voice would normally be soft. (You may have to practise doing this out of earshot.) Record your 'new' voice for comparison with your 'usual' voice. Observe the response in your pet or baby.

Q   Is it the same?

Q   Are these familiar communications recognised in exactly the same way?

If they are, then you have a very advanced baby or a very clever pet!

 For further explanations of the theory of phonology and practical learning activities:

Philip Carr, *English Phonetics and Phonology,* Blackwell 1999

M Davenport and S J Hannahs, *Introducing Phonetics and Phonology,* Arnold 1998

F Katamba, *An Introduction to Phonology*, Longman 1996

P Roach, *English Phonetics and Phonology*, CUP 2001

25 Understanding at word level

In classes for foreign learners of English, a lot of time is automatically invested in learning the sounds of the words.

Non-native speakers learn how each segment of sound is spoken in English; they learn where these segments, or **phonemes**[1] are spoken in the same way as in their own language, and they recognise where they differ.

When learning to speak the language they try to build up the syllables and then the words by beginning with accurate representations of these **phonemes**.

Speech and accent classes for native speakers of English approach segmental sounds in much same way, seeking to imitate the way each sound is uttered, and build from there.

Equally important in English is **word stress**, or the **syllable** of the word which is emphasised. Some languages are **syllable-timed** (see **sentence stress** p.71), meaning that the **stress**, or emphasis, is always

---

[1] For the reason of universal understanding, phonemic symbols are not used in any examples. Phonemically written examples of each phonological feature discussed here can be found in phonology reference books.

placed on a particular syllable in each and every word that is spoken. So imagine the difficulties this basic difference poses for newcomers to spoken English!

Word stress is automatically learned by native speakers, and is usually learned by non-native speakers as the pronunciation of the word is learned, so it may not be a serious hindrance to understanding.

Recognising the word in the context of an **utterance** is, however, crucial in understanding spoken English, and if the **stress** is placed on the wrong syllable of a word in connected speech, that word may be misunderstood.

Try this if you are a native or near-native speaker of English:

i   Write down a short sentence. Mark the **stressed** syllable in each word with a • above it. Speak the sentence while you read it, noting the **stresses.**

ii   Rewrite the sentence and mark the first syllable in each word with a •. Speak the sentence again, **stressing** only the syllables you've marked. Repeat this again **stressing** only the final syllables.

Native speakers of English

Should be aware that non-native speakers need to receive clearly spoken words within the context of each utterance in order to have a greater chance of accurate understanding.

Non-native speakers of English

Should be aware that it is just as important to learn words by their sound – both phonemes and syllable stress, as it is to learn how they are spelt, or indeed how the words are written phonemically.

26 Understanding the emphasis – sentence stress

Speakers of English use a series of signposts when they speak, to direct their listeners to the words that are most important, the 'information words'. It is this feature that makes English a **syllable-timed** language.

1   The problems

The rhythm of spoken English is largely dependent on which words are being **stressed** in each sentence.

This added level of emphasis causes a range of effects on the way the individual sounds and words that make up the whole sentence are spoken. As a consequence, understanding is more difficult for non-native speakers who are not aware of the 'emphasis on information' feature of English, or not familiar with the way stress changes the sound of individual words.

- Some words are linked together in a particular way because of their last and first **phonemes** and the way they combine in connected speech. This is called **assimilation**, and when it occurs the last **phoneme** may be lost and replaced by the first **phoneme** of the second word.

EXAMPLE: good boy - gooboy
good girl - googirl

- Some words become joined together, or **elided**, and small sounds are lost.

EXAMPLE: bottle of water - bollowater

- Some sounds are added, or **intruded**, to aid the smooth linking of two words.

EXAMPLE: there are - there'r'are

Non-native speakers of English

Should raise their awareness of the effects of stress timing on the sound and rhythm of the language, practising listening-recognition activities.

2   Using stress with awareness

Once the nature and purpose of **sentence stress** is understood, it can be a powerful communication tool. Adding extra emphasis to the words that the audience are supposed to hear – to the words that would already be **stressed** because they are the information words, or that should be **stressed** because they are the opinion words, adds clarity to the message.

EXAMPLE: The most important issue this year is definitely the environment, but I don't think that this issue is getting enough attention from this government.

⇨ **Try these:**

1   "Peter and Mary got married in Shrewsbury last Saturday."

Q   Where did Peter and Mary get married?

Answer the question using the complete sentence, **stressing** the word that gives the information needed.

"Peter and Mary got married in Shrewsbury last Saturday."

Q How many new questions can you make that can be answered using only the whole sentence and a single **stressed** word?

You should have been able to make five.

2 Take a short transcript (two or three sentences) of a monologue.

i Cross out the non-information words, like 'the', 'a', auxiliary verbs 'have' and 'be'. Speak the words you have left.

Q Were you still able to be understood by someone listening?

ii Using the same short transcript, eliminate all the information words and just speak the **grammatical** or non-information words.

Q   Could you be understood by someone listening now?

27 Understanding the 'music' – intonation

All languages use some form of musicality to add meaning to spoken communication. The voice rises ↗ and falls ↘ according to the meaning being expressed, and this is known as **intonation**.

In Drama and Speech studies **intonation** is also known as **inflection**.

One word can carry intonation, or moving **tone**, and the actual movement – whether it rises or falls – expresses meaning.

'Yes' said with a rising tone implies questioning – ↗

yes

'Yes' said with a falling tone implies a definiteness based on opinion or fact – ↘

yes

'Yes' said with a falling rising tone implies reservation or partial agreement – ↘ ↗

yes

Native and non-native speakers of English

Both native and non-native speakers of English should be aware that different languages may use tone in different ways on short answer words used to express these and similar functions, or meanings.

Where possible, it is a good idea for native speakers to find out about common intonation patterns if they are going to be communicating with people who speak a pre-known first language.

The English language uses **intonation** in four main ways:

- The **grammatical** way – for clarification when the actual **structure** of the sentence stays the same but can have two different meanings.

    EXAMPLE:
    ↘ ↗
    "Was he coming here before he left for the airport?"

    → ↘ ↗
    "Was he coming here before he left for the airport?"

- The **discourse** way – to focus the listener's attention on the key information, and indicate the kind of response expected.

EXAMPLE:

↗ ↘
It was last week that I saw him.

- The **accentual** way – to show the intended emphasis.

EXAMPLE:

↘
The last book of the series was very boring.

↗ ↘
The last book of the series was very boring.

- The **attitudinal** way – to show the opinion, or the speaker.

EXAMPLE:

↘   → ↗ ↘
I love your dress; it really suits you.

↗   →↗ ↗↘
I love your dress; it really suits you.

Native speakers of English

Should be aware that non-native speakers understand

what is being said with more accuracy if attention is paid to grammatical, discourse and accentual intonation, all of which provide useful pointers to key important information and appropriate responses.

Non-native speakers of English

A non-native speaker may have more difficulty understanding the nuances of attitudinal intonation, and may even use the same intonation pattern to express a different attitude in her / his own language.

Non-native speakers of English should be aware of the meaning inherent in intonation in English, and practise recognition activities whenever possible. It is advisable for non-native speakers to concentrate on acquiring intonation patterns through listening to and mimicking contextualised intonation, rather than transferring their own intonation patterns to English.

GLOSSARY

General terms:

L1	The mother tongue, or native, naturally acquired language
L2	The second, learned language
Linguistics	The study of the elements, composition and history of languages
Paralinguistic	Concerned with the study of linguistics, but in a non-academic way
Utterance	A group of words spoken together, that normally make sense

Language Structure:

Active and Passive	Two ways of composing a sentence - an active sentence clearly describes who or what is performing the action, and a passive sentence describes the action, but may not refer directly to the performer of that action
Communicative grammar	An approach to the study of grammar that is based on communicative meaning
Conditional	A sentence made of two clauses which talks about situation and outcome, or result
- condition clause	The clause describing the situation
- outcome clause	The clause describing the result
Direct and Indirect (Reported) Speech	Two ways of expressing speech - direct speech retells the speaker's words directly, usually using inverted commas to indicate this visually, and reported speech reports the words that were spoken, and may condense or summarise what was said

Function	The meaning an utterance or phrase conveys in the context of use, which is related to its structure (see also Structure)
Grammar	The study of the way language is structured, and what it means
Grammar system	The way in which a particular language is structured
Modal verbs	Auxiliary verbs used in future tense structures that add degrees of possibility and extend the range of functions possible for those tenses - will / shall / may / might must / should / ought to / can / could would
Structure	The way in which the words are put together in order to give meaning (see also Function)
Tenses	The structures that are used to show the time and duration of an action or state
- simple	Describes a single action or state
- continuous	Describes an action lasting over a period of time
- perfect	A tense, which uses the auxiliary verb 'to have' and describes an action in relation to another action or specific time
- future perfect	Describes a future action which is related to another future action or specific time
- past perfect	Describes a past action, which is related to another past action or specific time

Words:

Adjective	A word that describes a noun
Collocation	Two or more words that are usually expressed together
Idiom	A phrase that has a different, but commonly known meaning from its literal meaning

Lexis	Words - the words of a language
Lexical set	A groups of words with a common element
- morphological set	Words that have a common role in the grammar of the language
- semantic set	Words that have similar meanings
Noun	The name for an object, concept or person
Phrasal Verb	A commonly used verb phrase that is actually a preposition and a verb expressed together
Preposition	A word that is used in front of a noun to show time, location, manner etc.
Synonym	A word with a similar meaning to another word
Verb	A word that describes an action
- adverb	A word that describes the way the action is done
- reporting verb	A word that describes the way an utterance is spoken
Vocabulary	All known words, for example, by a person, or related to a specific occupation

Sounds:

Alliteration	Saying words consecutively that begin with the same first letter
Assimilation (Assimilated)	The way two words sound when spoken together, and the last sound (phoneme) from the first word and the first sound (phoneme) from the second word combine
Elision (Elided)	The way two words sound when spoken together, and the last sound (phoneme) is lost, or not sounded

Intonation (may also be known as tone / inflection)	The music of a language, the way the tone inflects, or rises and falls
- accentual	Using intonation to add meaning
- attitudinal	Using intonation to show attitude or opinion
- discourse	Using intonation to add grammatical emphasis
Intrusion (Intruded)	The way two words sound when spoken together, and an extra sound, such as an 'r' or a 'w', is inserted between the words
Phoneme	The smallest sound, combinations of phonemes compose all other spoken sounds
Phonology	The study of the sounds of a language
Stress	Spoken emphasis placed on syllables or words
- sentence stress	Emphases within a sentence
- word stress	Emphases within a word
- stress-timed	The rhythm of the spoken language is determined by variable word and sentence stress
Syllable	A single sound within a word containing the vowel sound
- syllable-timed	The rhythm of spoken language is determined by regular word stress patterns

PART 2
YOU AND YOUR VOICE

INTRODUCTION TO PART 2

Now that we have considered the tools that are used for communication, we must turn our attention to the instruments that actually do the communicating . . . . . you and your voice.

There are many books on the subject of voice and speech and we do not intend to make this a handbook of voice production.

There is comprehensive coverage of the subject in the companion handbook in this series *Preparing for your Diploma in Drama and Speech* by Kirsty N Findlay and Ken Pickering, so here, we are going to confine ourselves to a number of basic concerns.

Firstly, we need to remember that we begin communicating the moment we enter a room. The way we walk, arrange the furniture, stand in relation to other people or use eye contact, make an immediate impression on other people and they begin to make deductions about us before we have spoken a word.

We can establish the formality / or informality of the situation, convey a sense of relaxation / or tension, affect the 'atmosphere' or 'tone' of a meeting simply by our deportment and facial expression.

Once we begin to talk, a whole range of other factors come into play.

Q Do we sound friendly or aggressive?

Q Is our voice pleasant to listen to or irritating?

Q Do we sound confident and authoritative or nervous and tentative?

All these questions must be answered if we are to consider ourselves to be effective students of communication and this leads on to the next major point ..... the 'instrument' is our entire self!

It is vital that we find a way of taking total control of our bodies and ourselves to achieve that sense of focused energy that enables us to communicate with dynamism and skill.

<u>The underlying secret is to develop the power of relaxation and breathing.</u>

Breath is the very basis of our physical existence and it is no coincidence that the word for the inhalation of breath is **'inspiration'** or that this word is also rich with associations of 'spirit'.

Fortunately there has been a rediscovery in the West of some of the ancient forms of breathing and exercise developed in the East and you could do no better as a preparation for oral communication than to investigate Yoga or Tai Chi with their emphases on sustained breathing and total focus of energy.

The idea that the voice can operate as a separate entity had led to some absurdly exaggerated and elocutionary approaches to speaking that are both damaging vocally and embarrassing to listen to.

As a potential speaker, it is essential that you discover a relaxation sequence that you can use as preparation whenever a potentially stressful situation arises; and a great number of people are now finding help in the system of gentle body conditioning known as Pilates.

We know that we depend on our voices for much of our communicating. This precious and delicate instrument must last us for our entire lives and be able to respond to a wide variety of demands.

It is therefore essential that we care for the voice.

You can feel when your voice is being pushed too hard or when it is not being supported by adequate breath.

We should warm the voice up gently – like any other part of our body. We need to drink water constantly and avoid strain.

We should be aware that dry atmosphere, a sudden exposure to cold air or an audience arranged so that there is no hard surface behind it off which we can 'bounce' our voices, are all potentially damaging.

An audience or group confined in a space without proper ventilation is a nightmare for any speaker and a voice that is not carefully produced with forward-placed tone and adequate resonance will never hold attention or leave the speaker with any voice for the questions that might follow.

And then, of course, there is the question of nerves to consider . . . . . .

In this section, we are going to discuss what nervousness is and how it can work <u>for</u> rather than against you.

HARNESSING NERVOUSNESS AND USING YOUR VOICE

28 Nervousness

Many books report that the Number One fear people have is performance anxiety. Number Two is death.

"That means if you are at a funeral, you'd rather be in the casket than giving the eulogy."

Jerry Seinfeld

If you feel nervous about giving your first or fiftieth speech, you are in good company. Winston Churchill, Barbara Streisand and Paul Newman are three well-known people who have confessed to nervousness at the prospect of speaking in public.

Fear of public speaking has received quite a few descriptions over the centuries. It has been dubbed stage fright, glossophobia, communication reticence or speech anxiety at various times. Whatever the term, the feeling is familiar to almost anyone who ever gets up to face an audience.

Fear can take two forms:

> **physiological**

> **psychological**

Let's look at each.

29 Physiological basis for speech-fright

For most people, public speaking creates stress. Each of us is equipped with a stress mechanism that activates as soon as we perceive a threat. <u>Most stress is brought on by a lack of control.</u>

If you live in a cold climate you have probably had the experience of driving and suddenly losing control of your car because you hit a patch of ice. Your stress mechanism kicked in immediately you lost control. The pituitary gland located at the base of the brain automatically primed you for action. At the same time, your adrenal glands, located near your kidneys, started pumping blood through your body to give you the energy you needed to adapt to an emergency.

This stress mechanism can be a benefit, especially if it helps you ward off a threat. However, the mechanism can also produce an unpleasant physiological reaction. Your heart begins to beat faster and the blood surges through your veins. You might also break out in a sweat.

This physiological experience often disturbs public speakers the most. However, if you realise that your body is reacting to a potentially stressful situation, it shouldn't be such a problem. The problem occurs when you focus on the fear and the accompanying physical symptoms rather than your audience and what you are going to say.

Hans Selye, a pioneer in the study of stress, divides the stress reaction into two categories:

> **negative**

> **positive**

If you feel panicky for a long time negative stress can wear you down.

However, the same experience can also help you in a positive way. If you are excited about a particular event, like playing tennis or meeting a special person, the physiological reaction is positive.

These feelings also apply to giving a speech. Perceptions are important here. If you see the speech as intimidating and unpleasant, the stress will be negative.

On the other hand, if you are well prepared and have a desire to share your ideas with an audience, those perceptions will be quite positive.

30 Psychological reasons for stress

Austrian psychologist Alfred Adler proposed a theory called 'The Inferiority Complex'. Adler maintains that most humans, at one time or another, believe they're inferior.

This "inferiority complex" often results from the natural desire to be loved and approved. A normal amount of desire for approval is healthy. However, when the desire for approval becomes excessive, people who want too much approval set themselves up for failure.

If you analyse why people feel a great fear of public speaking, it usually boils down to an apprehension about making a fool of themselves. Very few people would get up to deliver a speech knowing the speech would be outstanding and then dread it.

Most people would relish the chance to do something well that makes them feel good about themselves. On the other hand if they perceive a situation that could make them look foolish, they'll most likely avoid it.

You might feel the same kind of fear walking into a crowded dance hall with the apprehension that you might become tongue-tied when talking to other people. If you know that you are going to meet new people and have them respond to you in a positive way, that experience can be gratifying.

Many speakers fear they will lose their place in an outline or manuscript, go blank and be unable to continue. One of life's less pleasant experiences is standing alone in front of an audience and not knowing what to say next. Less worrying but still unpleasant is a speaker's belief that she or he is boring and an audience doesn't really want to hear the talk.

31 The good news about nervousness – the energizer effect

If speech-fright can be unpleasant, it can also be a great asset if it is used properly. One of the most comforting phenomena for speakers is the 'energizer effect'.

The energizer effect occurs when three elements combine during a speech.

- the speaker is nervous

- an audience is present

- the speaker has carefully prepared

Those three factors blend to make the material more vivid in the speaker's mind. Ideas become better crystallized because the pituitary gland has been activated and adrenaline is pumping through the body.

Just the opposite occurs when a speaker is nervous, is facing an audience, but hasn't prepared. Then the mind tends to go blank because the stress mechanism kicks in.

Almost always, speakers who know their material well find that the material is more vivid in their mind when they're nervous.

Almost without fail, the speaker who doesn't know what he is talking about will find the material fuzzy because of the effects of this stress mechanism.

<u>Therefore, the only thing you have to fear is lack of preparation - not nervousness.</u>

32 Dealing with stage fright

- Accept the fact that stage fright is normal; you may have it every time you speak but let it work for you by thinking of it as excitement, not fear.

- Watch other people speaking and learn their techniques.

- Concentrate on your strengths to compensate for your weaknesses.

- Practise, practise, practise before you are going to present.

Remember, practice makes perfect presentations.

33 Managing the physical symptoms of stage fright

 For dry mouth:

➢ NO milk products, soda, or alcoholic beverages

➢ NO ice cream

➢ bite the tip of your tongue (this helps you to salivate)

 For sweaty hands/body:

➢ use talcum powder or corn starch

➢ carry a handkerchief

If you have red splotches on your face:

- wear pink or red colours
- wear high necklines
- use humour to release endorphins

 If your voice is shaky:

- project your voice to the back row of the audience

 If your hands are shaky:

- DON'T wave your hands about wildly
- gesture; then make small gestures

 If your legs are shaky or knees knocking:

- walk about the platform

 If your heartbeat is rapid:

- do some deep breathing
- avoid caffeine

34 Using your voice

"The manner of your speaking is full as important as the matter, as more people have ears to be tickled than understandings to judge."

Philip Chesterfield

Some speakers can talk about the most intriguing subjects but seem very dull because they speak in a monotone. Others can speak on relatively simple topics but they make their subject come alive. Outstanding speakers usually are adept at using their voice, as well as organisation and content.

➯ **You will need to be aware of at least five vocal elements:**

- **projection**
- **rate**
- **vocal quality**
- **inflection**
- **articulation**

35 Projection

Projection is a combination of volume and vocal energy.

The two are different. Some speakers can be loud but can still sound dull. Other speakers can talk softly but have such energy in their voice that they command our attention. The combination of the two is usually best.

When delivering a speech of your own, you will need to increase projection more than you think you should. Many speakers do just the opposite – because they are nervous, they tend to speak more softly than usual.

Projection during a speech has at least two advantages:

> **you sound more dynamic to the audience**

> **you re-channel physical nervousness**

Think for a moment about the process of projection.

To speak, you take a gulp of air and store it momentarily in your lungs. As you start to speak, the air leaves your lungs, travels up the trachea, strikes the vocal cords located in the larynx (the top of your larynx is your Adam's apple). From there the sound spreads through the three chambers of your throat, mouth and nasal passage.

If you are speaking softly, along with most speakers,

you'll probably experience the normal symptoms of nervousness, i.e. faster heart beat and muscle tension. Stronger projection will help dissipate those symptoms. <u>If you speak softly, you can literally feel the nervousness more acutely than if you speak with force.</u>

Always project your voice more than you think you have to. You'll sound better to the audience and you'll also feel less nervous. Projection does NOT mean that you shout or vocally badger the audience, but it does mean that you inject enthusiasm into your delivery.

36 Rate

<u>If speaking with more projection is important, so is speaking at a slower rate.</u> Most speakers tend to speak more rapidly than they should because of the adrenaline pouring through their bodies.

If you slow down, you can take advantage of the differential between thought speed and voice speed. While you typically speak at around 125 words per minute during conversation, your mind races at 400 to 500 words per minute. This allows you to listen to what the other person is saying, reflect on it, prepare a response and keep the conversation going.

The faster you speak, the harder it is to think ahead. If you start your speech at the rate 150 words per minute, it's hard to slow down. Tell yourself to speak at around 100 words per minute. Then you'll have more time to think about what you are going to say next and also time to focus on faces in the audience. Occasionally, student speakers will talk too slowly but the slow speaker is the exception.

To apply this point about slower rate, think of professional speakers like leading politicians and national figures. When you listen carefully, you'll notice that their rate is calm, measured, and relaxed. Many who speak rapidly sound tense.

As you mentally prepare for your talk, tell yourself that you are going to go slower than usual. When you practise with a friend or on a tape recorder or in front of a mirror, go slower. The rush of natural adrenaline during the speech will propel you to speak faster so any kind of slowing down process will probably help you.

⇨ **Try this:**

Some student speakers find it helpful to write SLOW

DOWN in capital letters at the top of each page of their outline.

37 Vocal quality

If projection helps tame speech-fright and rate gives you more control, then <u>vocal quality helps make your presentation sound more pleasant</u>. Most of us don't really know how we sound when we talk – even though everyone else does. Sound waves bounce off walls or run through our cranium and neither gives us an accurate perception of how our voice sounds to others.

If our voice is a primary index of our personality, the sound of the voice can either add to or detract from the effect we have on an audience.

Some people have voices that are warm and pleasant; others sound harsh and abrasive. We are usually more aware of someone who has a grating, abrasive voice.

An unpleasant voice may not have the same effect as screeching fingernails across the blackboard, but it can impact the overall effect of your speech.

The quality of your voice is a combination of several factors.

After a rush of air strikes your vocal cords, it disperses through your throat, mouth, and nasal passage. If those three chambers are constricted, you'll tend to have a higher sound than if you take full advantage of these natural amplifiers.

➡ Try this test:

Record your voice in a conversation or during a practice speech.

Q Do you like what you hear?

If you don't, there are ways to change the sound of your voice. Experiment by letting the sound roll around your nasal passage and mouth. Keep working at it until you are satisfied with the quality of your sound.

<u>Be careful that you don't become discouraged.</u>

Most people don't like the sound of their own voice when they first hear it, but with constant homework during conversation and practice on a tape recorder, they realise that the quality can be improved.

38 Inflection

Effective speakers sound enthusiastic about whatever topic they're discussing. Part of this stems from their vocal projection but they also use inflection well.

<u>Inflection is the vocal variety a speaker uses; and varied inflection is the opposite of a monotone</u>. Most good speakers use plenty of variety as they discuss a topic or give a speech.

Some speakers have very little vocal variety. These speakers can have the best ideas in the world, but if they transmit little vocal variety, an audience can quickly get bored.

39 Articulation

<u>Articulation refers to how distinctly a speaker enunciates words.</u> Articulation is NOT the same as pronunciation. If I mispronounce a word, I may put the accent on the wrong syllable or I may mangle the accepted usage.

If a speaker says, "I've just had a very unique experience", with emphasis on the first syllable of <u>ex</u>perience, he is mispronouncing the word.

Lack of articulation often includes slurring syllables,

which makes it difficult for audiences to understand what a speaker is saying.

Articulation is not an easy skill to develop or practise. Many of us speak with slurred diction in a conversation but it's harder to get away with that if you are giving a public talk. It is interesting to note that some professional speakers like Paul Harvey get away with speaking very rapidly because their articulation is so distinct.

 One of the best ways to improve articulation is to practise exercises that make you move your lips, mouth, and tongue with more vigour than usual.

Professor Henry Higgins in the musical *My Fair Lady* (based on the play *Pygmalion* by George Bernard Shaw) worked with Eliza Doolittle to improve her pronunciation and her articulation. He made her say "The rain in Spain stays mainly on the plain" over and over again until her words could be understood by the average British person.

Many professional speakers exaggerate pronunciation during a practice session. The practice helps them sound more distinct when they get in front of an audience.

40 Putting together all the vocal elements

Most effective speakers are able to blend all five elements (see Using your voice p.97) into a seamless vocal tapestry. They are energetic enough to sound interesting, they speak slowly enough to be easily heard, and the tonal variety is such that it's a pleasure to listen to what they're saying. Their voice quality is pleasant and they enunciate words clearly so that listeners don't miss a single syllable.

Professional speakers make it sound easy when they deliver talks <u>but what looks easy has taken years to develop and hone</u>.

Such speakers reflect the story of the traveller who arrived in London looking for the Royal Albert Hall. After half an hour, he noticed an elderly, stooped man with a violin case coming out of a doorway. He went up to the man and said, "Sir, can you tell me how to get to the Royal Albert Hall?" The little old man straightened up, raised his right fist and said, "Practise, practise, practise!"

You can practise every day during conversation. And the more you practise, the better your voice will sound to an audience. The rewards are well worth the effort.

PART 3

COMMUNICATION – CONTENT AND CONTEXT

INTRODUCTION TO PART 3

In this final part of our handbook we are going to bring together a recent and a very ancient approach to the study of effective communication:

➢ **The ideas of interpersonal communication**

➢ **The ideas of public speaking**

Modern social psychologists have grown increasingly interested in the ways in which human beings relate to each other and this has led them to investigate the various means by which we communicate.

This area of study can be of great benefit to both students and teachers who are anxious to develop communication skills.

Some time spent thinking about these matters will enable you to place your work in relation to an important body of theoretical understanding.

At the same time, the ancient arts of oratory and public speaking remain central to our civilisation and we can learn a great deal by exploring the principles that were developed long ago . . . . . and still serve as the basis for our work in effective communication today.

In PART 3 we shall be asking you to bear in mind both the content and the context of what you are attempting to communicate orally.

<u>All the highly developed vocal skills in the world will be of little use to you unless you have something significant to say.</u> Without this your work will be like so much of our modern world – all packaging and sub-standard content.

It will help you to remember that we are aiming 'for a sense that we are rewarding to be with, as people'. Those around us should feel that they are in contact with a mind, and a person who can both inspire and inform by what they say, and be equally adept at sympathetic listening.

You also need to appreciate that the style of communication and, indeed, the meaning of what you say will be profoundly affected by the context in which you are operating.

Linguists and literary critics, particularly, have demonstrated in recent years that <u>words do NOT have fixed and immovable meanings but that meanings are, in fact, constructed by listeners</u>.

This understanding should both heighten our sensitivity and ensure that we realise the complex nature of any kind of interpersonal communication.

Finally in PART 3, we are going to consider the results of all your hard study and practice.

 At the end of PART 3 there is a useful SPEECH EVALUATION FORM and PERSUASIVE SPEECH EVALUATION FORM for the evaluation of the performance of a speaker (see p.197 and p.198).

NOTE: You may be interested in this Effective Communication handbook because you are entering for an examination or assessment in Communication Skills or Speech. In order to make a success of this, or of any situation in which oral communication is vital, you must study and understand the criteria that are used to form a judgement on your performance.

Many colleges and organisations have developed criteria for the evaluation of this type of activity and, if you familiarise yourself with the ideas, guidelines and discussions that are developed by the assessors, you will be uniquely placed to achieve the standards expected of you.

Now, let's think about the ideas of interpersonal communication and public speaking in more detail . . .
. . . .

INTERPERSONAL COMMUNICATION

41 The experience of communication

Humans have a unique capacity to connect with others and communication is that linking mechanism.

They can experience joy, fun, excitement, caring, warmth, and personal fulfilment in relationships.

Because people are social animals, much of their happiness comes from effectively relating to other humans.

- The ability to co-operate with others and co-ordinate actions is important to both survival and professional success.

- The ability to form strong, healthy relationships helps people develop strong competent selves that can take care of themselves and others.

- Interpersonal skills are so important that there is no way in which we could overemphasise their importance.

The ability to share our experience and perceptions negotiating our realities with others is the essence of interpersonal communication.

Communication is all around you:

- **every day**
- **in everything we do and say**
- **in being with others**

From the moment you leap (or crawl) from bed in the morning to your final goodnight, you **communicate** to others.

From the first TV cartoon or radio talk programme in the morning to a goodnight kiss from a friend, you are also **communicated to**.

You experience communication, and you observe it from a distance. You understand it, and are confused by it. You accept communication, and reject it.

> "The uniqueness of man – the superiority of man in the world of animals . . . . . lies not in his ability to perceive ideas, but to perceive that he perceives, and to transfer his perceptions to other men's minds through words."
>
> Albert Einstein

42 Developing your communication potential and building your interpersonal style

In looking at the role of communication in daily life, it is important to look at how human beings have developed their abilities to communicate, and thus reach what linguist M A K Halliday called their 'semiotic potential' – the unique ability to create and understand meaning.

Your communication style has developed through experience and observation; and this development will continue throughout your life.

You first learned to communicate with the people around you as an infant. At birth (and, some even suggest, in the womb), you began the journey of life with the capacity for communication.

Soon after birth, you opened your eyes, cried when you were hungry or uncomfortable, smiled when you were content.

For the first 2 years, you relied on nonverbal messages:

- pointing
- stamping your feet
- making sounds

- hugging
- hitting
- crying

During this period you were practising language skills and learning the symbolic system and meanings.

By the age of 3, you had developed a good acquaintance with both verbal and nonverbal forms of communication.

Linguists point out that the language skills you developed during this period are among the most difficult learning skills you will master in your lifetime.

Much of your time in growing up has been spent building an effective personal style of communication.

- You have learned to sort out and communicate emotional states – distinguishing anger from disgust and sadness from hurt, for example.

- You have learned additional symbols:

  - slang phrases
  - second languages

- ➤ occupational jargon

- You have learned alternatives in responding to others' verbal and nonverbal communication.

- You have learned communication values:

- ➤ "How do I get what I want?"

- ➤ "When do I hurt others' feelings?"

- ➤ "When do I lie?"

An example can help put this process in perspective. If you have ever been around infants, you know they cry when they want to be changed or want attention. When children get a little older, they may have temper tantrums, (usually in a department store or some other public place) to get their way. However, an 18 year old who cried or had temper tantrums to get attention would be seen as socially immature.

- You have learned more subtle and socially appropriate ways to communicate needs.

- As you learned communication values, you were integrating your personality with ethnic and cultural background into personal style.

- And lastly, you have learned communication skills and strategies that you will use throughout your life.

For the most part, this learning has all been done informally, without the aid of a professional teacher. You evaluate what you learn, choose alternatives that work for you, and let others go. As you acquire new information and have new experiences, you modify what you have learned.

- Each new relationship teaches you a little more about your ability to communicate.

- Each group of friends builds expectations about you as a communicator.

- Each new setting requires a slightly different combination of your communication skills.

You modify your communication styles to accommodate your individual needs and requirements as well as societal norms for appropriate interaction.

The learning process helps you grow in ability to select the right communication skills, both in sending and receiving messages.

Once you build your basic communication style, you grow only through this process of evaluation and modification.

This book represents our effort as authors to encourage your continued self-evaluation and modification. We believe this book will help you to become the communicator you want to be by helping you reach your communication potential.

43   What is interpersonal communication?

To develop your interpersonal style, it is important to clearly understand what we mean by interpersonal communication.

Communication has been studied in Western cultures for more than 2,400 years. The humanistic study of communication as an art can be traced back to Greece and Aristotle's *Rhetoric and Poetics* written about 384 BCE.

The study of communication continued, with Roman rhetorical theory on the European continent and in Great Britain – and it has been studied in the United States of America for more than two centuries.

Interpersonal communication, as a separate study, grew out of scholars looking at communication as a social science, i.e. looking at the pressures, forces, or probabilities of what happens when humans communicate with each other.

This perspective on interpersonal processes began to emerge immediately after World War II.

The word **communication** comes from the Latin verb 'communicare – to share'.

The word **interpersonal** also has a Latin root and means 'between persons'.

Using these derivations as a base, we define **interpersonal communication** as a transactional process of creating shared meaning and building relationships with another person or persons.

The three critical concepts in this definition are:

1 transactional communication

2 shared meaning

3 relationship development

1 Transactional communication

In the work *Transactional Communication* (Wilmot 1987) communication is described as an ever changing, ongoing activity. This means that every element in the communication process is constantly changing:

➢ you change

➢ your communication partners change

➢ the environment changes

Throughout this non-static process, you are both a sender and receiver of messages and feedback.

2 Shared meaning

The notion of shared meaning refers to the idea that communicators are in constant negotiation with each other over the meanings of messages.

If you look at the definition closely, you will notice that we don't use the words 'intend' or 'intentionally'. This is because we believe communication can be both unintentional and intentional.

We don't believe that two people who communicate find the same meaning; instead, we believe that meanings are in the receiver (the receiver decides on the interpretation) and are negotiated between speakers and listeners.

3 Relationship development

The notion of relationship development refers to the idea that our communication has potential to build or destroy our connections with other people.

When we communicate interpersonally, we are essentially creating a relationship with another person. The continuous process of communicating allows us to build that relationship in a way that honours the changing, non-static, transactional process.

Even if the interpersonal communication leads to the termination of a relationship, it is interpersonal in that it took connections between people to negotiate that termination.

44 Culture

William Gudykunst (1989) has done extensive comparisons of cultural differences during a phase he calls 'uncertainty reduction' in communication with strangers. He has found that all cultures try to reduce uncertainty during the initial stages of a relationship but do so in different ways.

- Some cultures rely on the total context of the communication and rely more than other cultures on nonverbal signals and information about a person's background to reduce uncertainty.

- Other cultures rely more on verbal communication and ask specific questions about the person's experience, attitudes, and beliefs.

Q Which of these two methods of reducing uncertainty do you think would be considered appropriate for the Japanese?

Q What about the French or Swedish?

Q How about an Italian or African American?

Q Why do you think as you do for each?

Over time, interpersonal communication is dynamic and

ongoing rather than static – it becomes **transactional**. Although early encounters with others are normally impersonal, as people communicate over a period of time, they learn more information about each other. They are then able to predict and even explain the behaviour of their partners because the relationship has become increasingly interpersonal.

DeVito (1992) claims that as relationships grow more interpersonal the effectiveness of communication is characterised by the inclusion of the following qualitative elements (POSEE):

> Positiveness   A high regard for yourself and the other person, in which both state positive attitudes.

> Openness   A high degree of trust and honesty where self-disclosure can take place freely.

> Supportiveness   Communication that is characterized by descriptive rather than evaluative comments and by receptivity to each other's ideas.

- Equality   Not treating the other person, or letting the other person treat you, as superior or inferior, but rather as a respected equal.

- Empathy   The ability to put yourself in the place of the other person, to try to understand the world through his or her eyes.

DeVito believes that these five POSEE elements are interrelated and have equal importance. When they are not present in a communication encounter, the interaction is seen as non-interpersonal.

We can't give you a recipe for how you should communicate in all your relationships. Instead, our goal is to help you make wise, informed choices about communication as you learn about interpersonal communication through this Effective Communication handbook.

In that sense, this book is not prescriptive – we don't tell you what to do.

Instead, we are presenting you with information (theory) and practice that will help you make choices that are right for you.

We want you, as the student, to be active – prepared to wrestle with ideas that sometimes might go against your nature. We suggest new patterns of behaviour in this book to test alternate communication skills.

<u>Your involvement will be crucial to your growth and will sometimes have ethical consequences.</u>

Let's take a look at some ethical dimensions to see how they're part of the liberal arts tradition stressed in this text.

> "And ye shall know the truth, and the truth shall make you free."
>
> St. John 8:32

45 Ethical communication

Because interpersonal communication engages us with other people, you can influence others in positive and negative ways. For this reason, ethics becomes an important facet of interpersonal communication.

Johannesen (1990, p.1) writes,

> "Ethical issues arise in human behaviour whenever that behaviour could have significant impact on other persons, when the behaviour involves conscious choice of means and ends, and when the behaviour can be judged by standards of right and wrong."

<u>Ethical communication concerns itself with the well being of others, by demonstrating your sensitivity for their feelings and beliefs. Ethical communication expresses the truth and avoids deception or manipulation in relationships.</u>

46   Developing clear interpersonal ethics

It is important to communicate with integrity.

Q   What constitutes honest, ethical communication?

Q   What is manipulative and dishonest?

Ethics deals with what people may see as the grey

areas of life.

For example:

Q Is verbal deception ever appropriate?

Q Is a falsehood ever fair or just?

Q Can a lie end up doing something positive such as preventing harm?

Q Is telling the truth always a virtue?

Q Is it fair to hurt other people with actions and words?

Q Is it all right to use people for gain?

⇨ We suggest you keep a journal and create your own guidelines for ethical communication.

47 Interpersonal goals

Setting interpersonal goals can help you in your communication.

These goals can be realised only with your active

participation. Although you have been communicating since birth, and perhaps many times quite well, there may still be times when your communication seems to fall apart. Probably both your highest and lowest emotional moments in life centre on communication and relationships.

We want to help you find tools for looking at your communicative self and examining what is going on. We are NOT just suggesting new words for ideas you already have, or making a simple activity appear complex. We are talking about learning the fundamental concepts of communication.

48 Gaining self-knowledge

The first goal is to help you sensitise yourself to your personal communication strengths and weaknesses in your quest for truth.

⇨ Probe yourself.

Q What kind of person are you?

Q What do you want?

Q What do you need?

Q How did you get to be the way you are?

Q How does the person you are affect your communication behaviours?

Q Are you receptive to feedback?

Q Are you willing to change?

These questions and many more like them will help you to understand your **intra-personal self.**

49 Discovering commonality with others

The second goal is to help you develop skills for recognising your **commonality** with others.

Psychologist Carl Rogers (1970) suggests that what one thinks is most personal, is also often the most common.

> Rogers emphasises that as humans, we often experience the same joys and pains in life but we don't necessarily see others around us experiencing these emotions because we don't share our personal concerns with them.

50   Identifying the processes of communication

An additional goal is to identify and understand the essential elements of communication such as speaking, listening, feedback, messages and meanings, and perceptions.

You already have your own notions of what constitutes communication. You certainly recognise when someone seems to be communicating effectively or ineffectively.

Q   But could you say what the person is doing right or wrong in any particular communication encounter?

We would like to take the 'foggy' notions about communication behaviour, clarify them, and bring them back into a broader whole.

You can develop your own educated hunches or theories about communication by reviewing the major conclusions drawn from communication research, examined in the light of your own particular experiences.

51   Applying communication principles

The next goal is for you to apply this wisdom to your

own communication encounters, to evaluate your use of these principles or theories, once you have understood the theories discussed and have possibly even created some of your own.

These theories may reinforce what you already think or perhaps they might cause you to make some changes in your communication style.

52 Recognising basic elements of communication

The goal of recognising basic communication elements is to clarify the similarities and differences among communication situations and relationships so you can see the basic elements of each.

The key is to be able to apply your knowledge of communication concepts to whatever situation you are confronted with.

For example:

- comforting a grieving friend
- demonstrating a process at work
- meeting with a group about a concern you would like to take to your boss

53 Striving for quality

The final goal is for you to strive for quality in your communication experiences.

- Quality can be a product of all the goals we've listed.

- Quality can be achieved through conscious and consistent effort at improvement.

We share a basic assumption that communication is worth working on because it can be improved and that recognising the process and experience is the foundation for that improvement.

Suggested reading:

S Duck and R Gilmour (eds.), *Personal Relationships*, Academic Press 1981

This work looks at relationship development from a research perspective.

J A Jaska and M A Pritchard, *Communication Ethics: Methods of Analysis*, Belmont Wadsworth 1988

Jaska and Pritchard present an excellent survey of

ethical concerns in communication. The book also has many good ethical activities and a bibliography.

M L Knapp and A L Vangelisti, *Interpersonal Communication and Human Relationships*, Allyn and Bacon 1992.

Knapp's work on relational development has been important for many years. In this work, he and Vangelisti explicate the latest research on voluntary relational development in a clear fashion.

G R Miller and M Steinberg, *Between People: A new analysis of interpersonal communication*, Science Research Associates 1975.

In this classic text, Miller and Steinberg introduce the developmental approach to interpersonal communication.

J Powell, *Why am I afraid to tell you who I am?* Argus Communications 1969

Powell's book is an easy read that takes a humanistic look at self-disclosure in our relationships.

P Watzlawick, J H Beavin and D D Jackson, *Pragmatics of Human Communication,* Wilmot 1987

This work contains one of the foundational perspectives on the transactional nature of interpersonal processes.

ORATORY

54 The ability to talk effectively

At some time in our lives most of us try to influence the attitudes, opinions or behaviour of others. We use a range of techniques in our attempt to do this, but more often than not, <u>we use various kinds of talk.</u>

For the majority of people, this common activity takes place on a relatively small and modest scale, perhaps involving a few friends, family members, individuals or work colleagues.

Nevertheless, people, such as <u>entertainers, lawyers, politicians, religious leaders, teachers or sales staff aim at a much larger audience and must therefore develop their persuasive and communication skills accordingly.</u> Again, <u>the ability to talk effectively plays a major part in that repertoire of skills.</u>

However, it is almost certainly true that very few of us will be able to live our lives successfully without being able, if necessary, to speak well and persuasively in public.

In short, we need the art of oratory. This may be a somewhat daunting and even terrifying prospect but, in fact, oratory can be learned like any other skill and we are now going to concentrate on the art of making speeches.

We can learn a great deal about any skill from its great exponents. Oratory, the ability to use words skilfully in speech, is no exception. Every now and then, a human being has been born who has developed the capacity to change the course of history through their oratory and, although we might not expect to achieve anything so remarkable, we can learn a great deal about effective communication from such people.

You will find that the study of great orators makes one of the most fascinating areas of enquiry imaginable and you should take every opportunity to think about the styles and techniques of great speakers.

Investigation can provide us with insights into communication and also into ideas, prejudices and the nature of humanity itself. <u>It is difficult to over-estimate the sheer power and excitement of great oratory and its effect on civilization, as we know it.</u>

In a recent autobiography, for example, John Sergeant records how he was present at Dr Martin Luther King's great 'I Have a Dream' speech. That moment was a defining one in history and also in Sergeant's subsequent career as a radio and television political commentator.

Let's take another example and think about how someone changed the world through the spoken word. It was the remarkable speech by Thomas Huxley, in Oxford, England in 1860, that firmly established the idea that human beings had 'evolved' into their current condition rather than having been 'created' looking and behaving as they do now.

That debate continues today, and people debate it with as much passion now as when it was first mooted. However, it is very doubtful if the concept of 'evolution' as expounded by Charles Darwin in his book, *Origin of Species,* would ever have reached the level of public debate without the skilled oratory of Huxley. Darwin was painfully shy, and in an age when 'public lecture' or 'debate' was the predominant and crucial means of shaping opinion, he was at a great disadvantage.

At the conclusion of this section you will find an account of Huxley's speech (see p.145) and you should think through this example very carefully after considering the other points we now need to consider.

One problem for us now, in this present age, is that many of the greatest orators operated before there was any mechanical means of recording or technological means of mass communication available so we cannot know how great historical speeches were delivered.

Jesus Christ, for example, addressed huge crowds from a boat moored a short distance from the shores of lake Galilee. He influenced the lives of thousands, even in his lifetime, but we have to rely entirely upon the narrative of the four Gospels in the New Testament to gain an idea of the style and content of what he said.

Even if a recording of a great speech is available to us, we may have to use our imaginations to appreciate its impact on a live audience. Of course, a number of remarkable speeches have been especially devised for radio or television and these may be very different in style or intention from speeches delivered 'live' to a large audience.

For example, the President of a nation will adopt a totally different approach when addressing the nation in a radio broadcast after a natural disaster than when addressing the crowd at an election rally.

Some historians and a number of ordinary citizens, who lived in London during the Second World War, believe that it was only the radio broadcast speeches of the Prime Minister, Winston Churchill, that gave the British people the will to continue the struggle against Adolph Hitler.

However, listening to a recording of one of those speeches today, we need to understand a good deal of its context before we can really appreciate its original impact.

<u>We should certainly not imagine that the clue to effective speaking lies in attempting to imitate the very particular style of a powerful orator</u>.

We can, nevertheless, learn an enormous amount by analysing how various great speakers have achieved their results.

There are characters spanning the history of civilisation, up to and including the present day, who are remembered and known almost exclusively for their speeches. Their ability to affect the lives of thousands or even millions of people simply through what they have said and how they have said it should be of vital interest to any student or teacher of effective communication.

We may not see ourselves as likely to change the world in as dramatic a way but all of us try to impact on our fellow human beings.

We must constantly ask why great orators were so effective as communicators and attempt to discover some common features and general principles that we can use as we try to develop our own skills.

Unfortunately, we have to acknowledge that the results of skilled oratory are not always good. One supreme example of this is the fanatical following achieved by Adolph Hitler in the Germany of the 1920s and 30s.

Survivors of those terrible days expressed their views in a British television series, *The Nazis: A Warning from History,* and many who were greatly influenced by Hitler mentioned the persuasive power of his speeches.

Building on what many Germans considered to be an unjust peace treaty at the end of the First World War and an economic collapse, Hitler was able to incite intelligent, cultivated and 'civilised' people to express excessive nationalism, racial hatred and perform hideous acts of barbarism.

Footage of many of Hitler's speeches has survived and we can judge for ourselves the impact on the crowds he addressed. Indeed, it is a 'warning from history' that such things can occur.

Q Can you think of similarly shocking examples?

One of the problems of our 'post-modern' age is that there is so much cynicism towards politicians and other people in positions of authority. There is the constant suspicion that we are being manipulated. This is one reason why the historic expression 'rhetoric' that described the art of using oral language in a powerful and effective way, has now acquired a sense of surface reality and even deception. It is a great pity because, as we shall see, rhetoric was once and should still be, a major area of study.

Supporters of the American evangelist, Billy Graham, who has actually addressed more people 'live' than anyone else in history, would certainly want to argue that the same power that can be used for evil can also be used for good.

The ability to detect a mood, recognise a need, work on the emotional chemistry of a gathering of people and provide clearly articulated answers to what are seen as problems, are common and essential features of all successful public speaking.

Q But can we learn or teach oratory?

Certainly from ancient times it has been thought that the art of oratory can be acquired and in the next section MANAGING EFFECTIVE COMMUNICATION IN A VARIETY OF COMMUNICATION CONTEXTS we shall be introducing the laws of rhetoric by which this important skill can still be mastered. The famous fifth century theologian, St Augustine of Hippo, was primarily a teacher of rhetoric; so we can see how rich a tradition the modern teachers of communication have to build upon.

One of the most memorable examples of a student benefiting from the study of rhetoric is that of Queen Elizabeth 1 of England. When the queen was confronted with the impending invasion of the Spanish Armada, she personally addressed her troops in a famous speech at Tilbury. This inspirational piece of oratory was entirely based on the canons of rhetoric that she would have learned as part of her classical education; and this speech provided the much-needed stimulus for the English forces to engage a very powerful adversary.

It is almost certain that the speech in which the king rallies his troops against almost overwhelming odds in Shakespeare's *Henry V* is based on Elizabeth's speech.

We shall be introducing some of the laws of rhetoric and the way in which its principles still apply can be very helpful to us as public speakers (see p.161).

⇨ TRY THIS:

Think back over what we have been discussing in this section on oratory. Then respond to these questions:

1   Here are two controversial statements. Discuss or reflect on them and provide evidence to support or attack the following statements:

    'In fact, very few of us will be able to live our lives successfully without being able, if necessary, to speak effectively in public'.

    'Rhetoric was once, and still should be, a major area of study.'

2   Think of two speakers who have amassed a

large group of devoted followers as a result of their abilities as a public speaker.

3   What physical and vocal qualities do you associate with a great orator?

4   What are the problems involved in trying to assess an orator from the past?

5   The scene is the annual meeting of the British Association for the Advancement of Science, held in Oxford in 1860. Among the speakers are the Bishop of Oxford, a well-known anti-Darwinian and Thomas Huxley, Darwin's supporter.

Here is a description of what happened:

The Bishop rose, he was an effective speaker and had an excited audience. Those on his side no doubt thought he was marvellous. One of those on the other side said he 'spouted for half an hour with inimitable spirit, ugliness and unfairness'. He was, at first, jovially amusing and then brutally scoffing. He ridiculed Darwin's 'proofs'. But then he went too far. Having reached his triumphant peroration, he descended to cheap ridicule. Turning to Huxley he asked whether it was through his grandfather or his grandmother that he claimed his descent from a monkey. Huxley was, at first affronted, but then he delightedly struck his knee and whispered to his neighbour, "The Lord hath delivered him into my hands!" He rose, pale and impassive. He achieved his effect by a contrasted quietness. He soberly defended Darwin's theory. Then he became even more quiet and grave. He would not, he said, be ashamed to have a monkey for an ancestor, but he would be ashamed if his ancestor were a man 'who prostituted the gifts of culture and eloquence to the service of prejudice and falsehood'. There was an instant commotion. One lady is said to have achieved minor fame by fainting.

Now consider these questions:

i Why was Huxley's response to the Bishop so effective?

ii What did Huxley mean by 'The Lord hath delivered him into my hands', and what is the irony of his saying this?

iii What factors influenced this early debate on evolution?

iv Why do you think so graphic a description of this event has survived?

MANAGING EFFECTIVE COMMUNICATION IN A VARIETY OF COMMUNICATION CONTEXTS

55 Preparing a speech for a known audience

Many people find themselves in the unexpected, and perhaps unwelcome, position of having to "give a speech" at some time in their lives. The occasion may be a wedding, christening, school reunion, club function, training session at work, or a similar context in which the speaker normally knows the topic s/he will be speaking about, and the type of people who will be listening.

The speech-giver can ensure that s/he is confidently addressing the three fundamental questions – **'What?'**, **'Who?'** and **'Why?'** by following a few simple rules of preparation.

NOTE: The model of preparation in this section is a useful basis for all types of public speaking, and can be developed in more detail in different contexts, such as public speaking to an unknown audience, which is discussed next (see p.154).

<u>The success of all forms of public speaking depends, to a great extent, on the quality of the preparation</u>. Knowing the audience and being familiar with the content of the speech does NOT reduce that dependence. On the contrary, if anything, familiarity emphasises the importance of meeting, and even

exceeding the expectations of the audience. A lot hangs on your speech; after all, if you know these people, you will probably see them again in the near future!

Preparation Stage 1

The first stage of preparation should give the speaker a clear sense of context and direction.

➡ Ask yourself the following questions:

- THE AUDIENCE

    Q Who are they?

    Q Why are they listening to me?

    Q What can I say that will be interesting to them?

    Q What can I say that will be useful for them?

- MY OBJECTIVES

    Q What key message do I want to give my audience?

Q   What kind of response do I want?

EXAMPLE: Emotion or action?

Q   What kind of tone do I want to communicate?

EXAMPLE: Informative, amusing, persuasive, entertaining or inspirational?

Preparation Stage 2

The second stage of preparation involves clarifying and logically ordering the key points of your speech.

➡ Use this process:

i   Summarise the message in one sentence.

ii Write an introduction:

   (a) which reiterates the key message

   (b) which outlines your purpose

   (c) which establishes contact with the audience

iii Check the introduction to make sure it achieves these objectives.

iv   List the main points of your topic, argument or discussion in logical progression, making a key-point plan.

v   Find relevant examples for each main point, and insert them into the relevant places in your key-point plan.

vi   Prepare 'links' to join your main points together, and insert them into the relevant places in your key-point plan.

NOTE: The use of questions as links helps an audience to summarise what has been said, and interact with your theme.

vii Summarise your main points into a meaningful conclusion.

viii Prepare a final, thought-provoking sentence that should challenge the audience to both remember and interpret what you have said.

NOTE: The final sentence is of vital importance and must be memorable. In this way your speech will be recalled - even if you are followed by a number of subsequent speakers.

If you have followed this preparation plan, the outline of your speech should look like this:

- OBJECTIVE

- KEY MESSAGE

- INTRODUCTION

- MAIN POINTS:

    POINT 1 + RELEVANT EXAMPLES

    link

    POINT 2 + RELEVANT EXAMPLES

    link

    POINT 3 + RELEVANT EXAMPLES

    link

- SUMMARY

- CONCLUSION

- FINAL STATEMENT

Preparation Stage 3

i   Do not write out the speech verbatim. Instead, use point form notes based on your model to encourage fluidity in your expression.

ii   Rehearse for timing. Make sure you don't have to rush to cover all your points, or to expand and ad-lib too much to fill in time.

iii   Rehearse for quality of expression, and make the necessary changes that will give your speech maximum impact (see PART 1).

Q   Which words do you need to stress when speaking?

Q   Which sentences have become too complex?

Q   Which words, phrases and illustrative examples are not accurately pitched at your audience?

> With such careful consideration of the context, rational and ordered delivery of the relevant points and examples, and the final lucid, thought-provoking conclusion, there is no reason for your speech not to be a success!

56 Speaking to an unknown audience

Now that the basics of speech preparation have been established in the context of addressing an audience known to you, about a subject in which there is shared interest and prior knowledge, we can move to the more challenging, and perhaps even more intimidating, situation of giving a prepared speech in an unfamiliar context.

You may have been invited to speak by an organisation about which you know little. You may be preparing for an examination, or you may even have decided to take up after-dinner speaking!

In each of these situations, the basis of common interest cannot be assumed – you, the speaker, must create it.

57 Choosing a topic

This may seem easy at first, but for many speakers it is arguably the most difficult part of speech preparation.

Q   Do you pick a subject you're familiar with already or do you plunge into something unfamiliar?

That decision is up to you, but in general the less time

you have to prepare, the more advantageous it is to pick a topic that you are somewhat familiar with already, and that you think your audience may know something about, as well.

➪ Brainstorm - to generate as many topics as possible.

At this stage, try not to be critical of your ideas but rather generate a list of as many topics as possible.

Four criteria helpful in this process are:

- your interests
- your knowledge
- your audience's interests
- your audience's knowledge

If you have no interest in the topic, you won't deliver the speech with conviction or enthusiasm. On the other hand, if you speak about something that you are interested in but you believe your audience isn't, you will need to find a way to gain their interest. It is also very difficult to speak about something you or your audience has little knowledge about. By keeping these four considerations in mind, you can come as close as possible to generating a topic of interest and value to everyone.

58 Analysing your audience

Before you get heavily into researching your topic, make sure you analyse your audience. Ask yourself about the age and knowledge level of your listeners.

Q   What attitude might the listeners have towards the topic?

Q   What emotional response to the topic do you expect of the listeners you are going to address?

If you are thinking about giving a speech advocating pro-life, for example, you can predict that a number of audience members will favour your stance on the subject, but you can also predict that a number will not. In addition, some people may be neutral about the topic.

For a persuasive speech, the more you know about audience attitude, the better chance you have of motivating people to accept the stance of

the speech.

If you are preparing a talk on banning smoking in public places to an audience of smokers, for example, you should think again! Pick another topic so you avoid what some researchers call the "boomerang effect" when you harden people in their attitudes merely by presenting the subject rather than motivate people to accept your position.

Ideally, you would want to take a survey to assess the attitudes of the members of an audience, but that's nearly always impractical.

At the very least, stop and think about how the audience may react to your subject.

59 Researching your topic

Conducting research sometimes presents us with the daunting challenge of where to begin. Think of research as trying to get answers to your questions. Good research starts with good questions.

One tool of research is the interview. Once you have chosen the interviewees, you need to prepare your interview questions. Remember to include both open and closed questions.

Open questions require opinion, explanation and description from your interviewee, and the unpredictable nature of the answers may provide colour for your speech.

Closed questions require 'yes' and 'no' answers, and may be used to check facts without wasting interview time.

It is also crucial to take ordered, legible notes, and accurate quotes when they seem appropriate to your theme or topic.

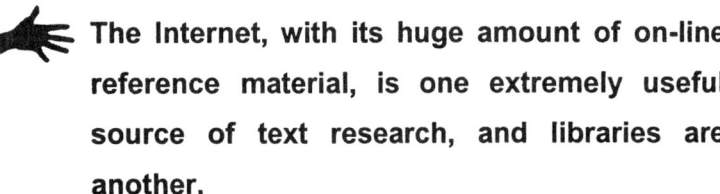 **The Internet, with its huge amount of on-line reference material, is one extremely useful source of text research, and libraries are another.**

When conducting research, think of an hourglass as a metaphor for your strategies. You should start broadly, with general references, then narrow your search with specific journal articles or books on your topic, and finally broaden the conclusions or generalisations you can draw from your research.

Just as note taking is important in an interview, it is equally important when researching reference texts. Few things can be more frustrating than trying to find a source that you used but from which you took inadequate notes at the time.

⇨ The minimal information you write on a note card should include:

- Author, title, date, and publisher

    NOTE: The ISBN number is also useful in library research, in case you have to find the reference again.

- Page numbers of article

- Any quotations, copied verbatim

- A summary of the main ideas in the text

Keep all your note cards from interviews, the Internet and library research. Some public speaking contexts may require an accurate bibliography of the resources you consulted. Even if this isn't needed for the speech you are giving, you may use the speech again, in a different context, where references are needed.

60 Putting your speech together

▭▷ Use this plan:

i **Write an outline based on what you already know about the topic.**

Start with your key sentence – the main point of your speech, and then break this down into three main points. The outline can then be constructed around these points.

ii **Think about a specific introduction that will get the attention of the audience now that the main body of your speech is prepared.**

The introduction must establish your credibility on the topic, establish a rapport with your audience, and point out the direction you intend to go in your speech. Typical introductions can include stories, challenges or quotations.

NOTE: Brief stories that relate directly to your topic always work well because they follow a chronological order and are easy to remember. Almost everyone will listen to a good story, if it is entertainingly told.

iii **Write the conclusion.**

We have already seen that a conclusion serves two purposes. It summarises the key points of the talk and ties everything together - preferably with a compelling final sentence.

If you memorise just one line of your speech, make it the concluding sentence. Some speakers hover like a plane trying to find a landing strip before they conclude their speech! Conclusions should be specific and should leave the audience with a memorable thought about the theme.

For example the conclusion of a motivational talk on the importance of self-image and how one's thoughts shape the feeling of confidence could finish with a quotation from Henry Ford: "Whether you believe you can or believe you can't, you're right."

61   Remembering your speech

- Trust a well prepared outline rather than a memorised script.

- Use vivid imaging to remember the key points of your outline.

Words by themselves tend to be abstract and hard to remember, whereas clearly grafted images in your mind are far easier to recall, especially if they're in outline form. If you vividly imagine the setting and audience for the speech before you arrive, and then use effective memory techniques, you will speak with confidence.

Some public speaking trainers suggest taking the key ideas from your outline and putting them on note cards. The idea is that if you know the material well, but don't try to memorise every word, you will be in greater control.

62   Using memory techniques

Treatises on memory have been around for a long time. In his book *De Oratore*, the first century Roman politician and well-known speaker Cicero discusses various ways to remember speeches.

Over the centuries, many other experts have offered helpful tips for speakers who want to have control over their material. Let's look at some of these **memoria technica** or memory techniques.

63 How the memory works - vivid imaging

The mind is an amazing mechanism. Not only can we think, but the central nervous system also allows us to remember events from the past.

Faculty psychologists of the 19th century used to divide the human mind into compartments - one for cognition, another for memory, and another for sensing, and yet another for sight, etc.

More recent research has shown that the human mind is much more complicated than that and often cognition blends into imagination. However, for the purpose of explaining the vivid imaging system, we can make a distinction between cognition and imagination

When you think about an abstract concept, you don't necessarily have to have an image in your mind. For example, when someone says, "loyalty is a virtue" you understand the meaning.

Other cognitive type statements include:

- five plus seven equals twelve

- honesty is the best policy

- Jean Paul Sartre was an existentialist

- women often make better leaders than men

- reading is a more complicated process than watching television

You can understand those abstract thoughts, but you will remember them much better if you form a vivid image of each one.

Think of a film you've seen recently - or even a year ago. If someone asked you to describe the plot and the characters, you could probably do so easily. You form pictures in your mind. This is what we mean by "vivid imaging".

Vivid imaging is a process of clearly seeing in your imagination a scene before it occurs. Imagination is different from intellect. Our intellect allows us to think of abstract ideas like the ones listed here. Our mind can make the connection between the two ideas, but it's hard to form a picture.

For example, the statement "the car was in an accident" is less difficult to understand than the statement about Jean Paul Sartre, but it is still abstract. If you were asked to imagine a Rolls Royce slamming into a telephone pole, you would probably remember it more easily. If you were shown a picture or a video of a car crashing into the pole and then asked you to remember it five minutes later, you would recall it even more vividly.

The more you use your imagination along with your thoughts, the clearer the material will be to you. Let's apply that to giving a speech.

If you were asked to think of yourself before you deliver your talk as calm and prepared, you could do that. However, if it were suggested that you vividly imagine yourself walking from your chair to the podium, and pausing, before starting with a very specific introduction, you would have a better chance of remembering the process.

Abstract ideas are like Teflon - they often don't stick. If you use the Velcro of vivid imagination, you can remember concepts much better.

There are two ways you can use vivid imaging to help you deliver an effective speech. The first, **long-range preparation** - relates to advance preparation and the second, **direct preparation** - can be applied to remembering the key ideas in your talk.

64 Long-range preparation

When you know the date and venue of your talk, imagine yourself as somewhat nervous but in total command because you have prepared so thoroughly. Vividly imagine yourself walking to the front of the room addressing the audience, establishing eye contact and talking with expertise on your subject. Some people find it helpful to meditate in the few days before they give a talk. Meditation will help you to focus and reduce stress.

The following tip may appear negative at first, but many professional speakers find it helpful.

Imagine in advance the worst that could happen when you deliver a talk. The majority of people think the worst experience would be going blank and not knowing what to say next. Play out in your mind what you would do if you go blank. See yourself pausing for a few seconds, looking at your outline and finding out where you were, and then continuing to speak. In the unlikely event that the worst happens, you have a plan.

65 Direct preparation

You are now ready to apply vivid imaging to direct preparation. Remember that the more you use your imagination, the better chance you have of mastering the material for your talk. If you have been impressed with people who have a superb memory, they probably use three basic methods:

> ➢ **association**
>
> ➢ **imagination**
>
> ➢ **repetition**

Association is a linking of vivid images in your mind and repeating them enough times so you remember them well.

An example of this process might be helpful. Suppose someone asked you to try to repeat the following unrelated listed items: the film character ET, a yellow Volkswagen, a pine tree, a telephone pole, a brick, a cup of coffee, blue suede shoes, broken glass, an angry librarian, a spiral staircase and a glass door.

Q Could you easily repeat the list of items?

The answer is, probably not.

➪ **Now try this:**

Picture in your mind, as graphically as you can, the character ET from Steven Spielberg's film. Now see ET driving a yellow Volkswagen in front of a library. He parks his yellow Volkswagen between a pine tree and a telephone pole. On the passenger seat is a brick. ET picks up the brick, gets out of his Volkswagen, goes up the steps of the library, comes to the glass door and hurls the brick through the glass door. A librarian is sitting behind the glass door wearing blue suede shoes. Behind this person is a spiral staircase. The brick crashes through the glass door striking the coffee the librarian is drinking and it spills all over his blue suede shoes. In anger, the librarian picks up the brick and throws it back at ET who scrambles down the steps littered with broken glass and leaps into his yellow Volkswagen, which is still parked between a pine tree and a telephone pole. He then drives off.

If you try repeating that series of images two or three times, notice how much easier it becomes to talk about it. You have applied the principles of memory. You linked a number of vivid images and then repeated the series so that the images became firmly entrenched in the memory section of your mind.

Another technique that reinforces this method is to

highlight those words that are the most vivid in your imagination, so that if you are speaking and you momentarily forget where you are, you can glance at the outline and the highlighted words will stand out from the others on the page.

66 Rehearsing the speech

Public speakers can use a variety of speech rehearsal techniques:

o   Some like to practise in front of a mirror, but others may find this approach artificial. A more realistic method is to deliver the speech to family member or friend.

o   Some use the technique of recording the speech and playing it back a number of times until they have a solid grasp of the material.

o   Some play out in their mind the scene of the talk and then mentally connect the various images they're going to discuss.

Use whatever approach you find works for you, but make sure you practise your speech at least three to five times before the big day.

67 Humanistic and cross-cultural considerations
– helping your audience to listen effectively

Effective communicators must also be good listeners, and accurate judges of the potential for aural comprehension, and the receptiveness of their audience or listeners.

The speaker is not communicating the message to his / her audience, be it an individual in a two-way conversation or a hall full of people listening to a public speaker, if any of the following are occurring:

(a) The listeners are finding it difficult to follow what is being said.

(b) The listeners do not understand what is being said.

(c) The listeners are bored and feel uninvolved in what is being said.

The job of the effective communicator is to ensure that his/her message:

- is pitched at the right level

- includes references such as illustrative examples that have meaning

- actively seeks a response, be it internal or vocalised, from the listeners

▷ **Try this:** (see Glossary p.79 for an explanation of specific terms)

Imagine yourself in two listening roles; that of a native speaker listening to your own language, and that of a non-native speaker listening in your second language.

1   As a native speaking listener, think back to the various occasions when you have been listening to speakers.

i   Then check each of the L1 BARRIERS IN LISTENING SITUATIONS to identify difficulties you might have experienced.

ii Put a tick against each situation you identify. Then, think back to at least three occasions when you had this difficulty. Try to include a time when you were actively part of a one-to-one or small group conversation, and also a time when you were part of a passive audience.

iii In each situation, think specifically about what the communicator could have done to maximise the accuracy of your listening.

L1 BARRIERS IN LISTENING SITUATIONS

(a) Your emotional response to what was being said caused you to become distracted and you consequently misunderstood.

(b) You had pre-conceptions about what would be said, and this caused you to misunderstand the information being given.

(c) The speaker deviated from the main point in a way that you found illogical, and you lost the thread.

(d) The speaker used complex grammar and vocabulary that did not communicate his / her meaning directly, leaving you feeling confused.

(e) The speaker progressed through the topic extremely slowly, and you became distracted.

2 Now, as a non-native speaker, think back to the occasions when you have been listening to speakers using your second, or other languages.

i   Check the three L 2 BARRIERS IN LISTENING SITUATIONS to identify difficulties you might have experienced.

ii Again think about how the speaker could have helped you as a listener to understand what was being said more accurately and effectively.

L 2 BARRIERS IN LISTENING SITUATIONS

(a) In a group or passive audience situation, the speaker was speaking too fast and you couldn't keep up with the pace.

(b) The speaker used many words with which you were unfamiliar, and you lost the thread of the speech.

(c) The speaker used more complex grammatical structures than you were used to, and you couldn't understand what was being said.

68 What listeners can do - understanding listening from the audience's perspective

Listeners, both native and non-native, can be trained, or can train themselves to listen more effectively. You may wish to train your own listening skills, or those of a group you regularly speak to. Even if you don't have the opportunity to train your listeners, you can incorporate some of these points into your own communication preparation:

- In a one-to-one or small group conversation ask questions to check understanding.

- As a 'passive' audience member summarise the speech into a number of key points while the communicator is speaking.

- Use 'Who', 'What', 'Where', 'When' and 'Why' questions to keep track as the speaker moves through the topic.

- Make brief notes – as this can be invaluable in a 'passive' listening situation.

- Use the context of what is being said to understand unfamiliar words. Pay attention to the speaker's use of adjectives, adverbs and reporting verbs to gain greater understanding of his/her opinion.[1]

---

[1] See The power of words – choosing and using words carefully p.54.

- Think of grammar as a communicative tool that carries meaning. Actively use grammar to gain greater understanding of the finer points of what is being said, and the opinion that is being communicated through the choice of modal verbs and conditionals.[2]

- Listen to the speaker's tone of voice. Then question yourself about the way the speaker is delivering the speech[3].

    EXAMPLE:

    Q What is the pitch?

    Q Which words are being emphasised?

    Q Where does the speaker alter pace?

- Interpret the speaker's message and form opinions about what you hear, as you listen.

    NOTE: Even in a 'passive' listening situation the listener can respond actively, if internally.

---

[2] See LANGUAGE STRUCTURE p.18.
[3] See SOUNDS p.66.

69 Using the tools of communication effectively

In PART 1 the roles of the tools of communication were analysed in some detail. The elements of oral communication i.e. the effect of sentence structure, words and sounds – were considered in terms of their effect on both native and non-native English speakers.

In any situation where you are managing effective communication – anything from speaking to a large group in a public hall to managing a round-table group discussion, you need to consider how you are using the tools of communication, and whether you are maximising their potential.

It is even more important to use these tools wisely when there are non-native speakers, or English speakers from different English speaking countries, in the audience or group, when listening competence and/or expectations can vary.

Points to remember:

- Always choose your words carefully, keeping in mind the way in which they reflect your own opinions and the level of potential understanding in the majority of the audience. Remember that there are many meanings for the same word in the English language, and many choices of word for the same meaning, and this can be particularly confusing for non-native speakers.[1]

- Use sentence structure effectively to express your meaning as exactly as possible. When making a key point, use the simplest sentence structure possible, and re-formulate it in another sentence structure when re-iterating the point.[2]

- Use your voice as a tool of communication; maximising the potential of word stress, or emphasis, and intonation, or inflection, to add depth to your meaning.[3]

- Keep your audience involved. Use references and examples that have direct relevance to them, pose questions around key points as you move through the topic, use your body expressively, make eye contact with individuals in larger audiences, and make sure that you don't wander from the theme of your communication. Asides and in-jokes may be amusing to those in the know, but they are

---

[1] See WORDS p.54.
[2] See LANGUAGE STRUCTURE p.18
[3] See SOUNDS p.66.

often frustrating if not annoying for the uninformed who are likely to feel excluded.

- When communicating to a small group, such as speaking in a seminar, use concept-checking questions at regular intervals in order to gauge understanding, and check that the members of the group are following your line of argument. This is particularly important when non-native speakers are listening, so you can ensure that they have understood your exact meaning.

  NOTE: The concept-checking questions should ask for key information rather than merely requiring a one word 'yes' or 'no' answer.

- In small group communications remember that English speakers have a habitual tradition of interruption for turn-taking, while other people who speak languages such as Japanese or Finnish wait until the speaker has stopped, even in an informal one-to-one situation. When managing multi-cultural group conversations, ensure that everyone has the opportunity to speak or to question, since some may not make that opportunity for themselves.

- Research the types of responses that you can expect before communicating with a multi-cultural audience. Remember that people of different cultures listen in different ways. People of some cultures feel it acceptable to interrupt and ask questions in any communication context while others listen in absolute silence, even in a small group situation, because to do anything else would be rude.

- Ascertain the listening purpose of your audience.

Q Do they wish to gain information?

Q Do they wish to be entertained?

Q Do they wish to be persuaded?

Q Are they reluctant to receive your message?

Structure your speech to match the purpose and possible receptiveness of the audience, as well as achieving your own communication goal. You should also seek to involve the reluctant, entice those who need to be persuaded or entertained, and give an unambiguous message to those needing facts.

70 In conclusion

In this MANAGING EFFECTIVE COMMUNICATION IN A VARIETY OF CONTEXTS section, we have given you preparation guidelines that will help you to be effective in any type of public speaking. You now have tools for remembering and rehearsing your public speeches, an understanding of communication from the listener's perspective, methods for maximising effective listening in any communicative situation, and a relevant analysis of how sentences, words and sounds affect comprehension.

You should now be able to prepare and deliver a speech for any type of audience, and manage the dynamics of small group communication . . . . . and hopefully enjoy it, too!

NON-VERBAL FACTORS IN SPEECH DELIVERY

71 The elements of non-verbal communication

Delivering a speech requires more than having a well-written speech and effective use of your voice. A speech is also judged on the ethos or credibility of the speaker.

Many factors contribute to create a credible speaker and we would like to focus on four specific elements of non-verbal communication here:

- **dress**
- **posture**
- **gestures**
- **audio-visual aids**

72 Dress

You have done the preparation for your speech, so now it is time to consider your appearance, as you get ready to deliver your speech.

Q   What should you wear?

Remember that the way you look has a direct impact on your audience, especially when you start to speak. Anything that distracts can affect your performance –

an untidy shirt hanging out, a loud outfit or dirty, ripped clothes, for example, can create a negative effect.

The appropriateness of dress is a good starting point when considering what to wear.

It is important to think about the type of venue where you will be speaking, and the type of event. Ask yourself:

Q What types of people visit this venue?

Q How do these people dress?

Q What is appropriate dress for this occasion?

You should aim to fit in, and look smart and purposeful within that environment.

In addition, your own objectives in giving your speech must also be taken into consideration when you are thinking about what to wear as these are of even greater importance. Ask yourself:

Q Do you wish to persuade?

Q Do you wish to inspire confidence?

Q Do you wish to sound knowledgeable?

If so, you need to 'look the part'. Think about the expectations your audience would have of a speaker with your objectives, and dress to fit the bill.

73 Posture

Stand straight, tall and confident, even if you don't feel that way at first.

- **Avoid slumping or hunching your shoulders**
- **Try not to pace back and forth unnecessarily**

While some speakers feel more comfortable sitting on the front part of a desk to project a more casual look, it is probably advisable to begin standing straight, and control your movements and stance in a way that is appropriate to the speech you are giving, and the expectations of your audience.

If you, the speaker, project assurance through your own posture, your confidence will hold the attention of your audience.

74 Gestures

One of the more colourful eras in public speaking was the 'Elocutionary Period' in the late 1800s. During this time, teachers of speech emphasised the exaggerated use of gestures for public speakers. Students had to describe exactly what gesture they were going to use on what syllable of a particular word.

We are not suggesting that you follow these Victorian dictates here in this Handbook!

However, we do want to provide a few simple guidelines for using gestures.

Speakers can distract an audience - either because they use awkward, exaggerated gestures or because they use virtually no gestures at all.

In the first instance, a speaker might be waving wildly or pointing an index finger at the wrong time.

At the other extreme, a speaker might stand stiffly facing the audience with both hands clutched in front, held behind the back or tucked in both pockets of a jacket or trousers.

As a basic rule, any non-verbal cue that distracts, or does not have a specific communicative objective, should be avoided.

Any gesture that reinforces what you are saying is appropriate.

75 Audio-visual aids

You have now prepared your speech by putting it in outline form.

Q What about using audio-visual aids?

The answer to that question of course depends on the kind of speech you are giving and what visual aids might help make your talk more clear or persuasive.

You can strengthen almost any kind of speech with audio-visual aids.

➪ Let's look at some of the advantages.

Highlighting your speech with visual aids tends to make the material stick longer in the minds of the audience. If, for example, you were giving a presentation about Napoleon's defeat at Waterloo in 1815, your audience would be far more likely to remember what you said if 'told and showed' what happened to the beleaguered French commander, using a picture of him and a map where the battle was fought.

76 Types of visual aids

There are a variety of audio-visual aids available to you that are apt for a speech on almost any topic.

REALIA

Realia can be an interesting way to illustrate and demonstrate what you are saying providing the objects can be easily seen by the audience and used by the speaker.

If you were demonstrating how to swing a golf club, for example, you could bring along two or three clubs and a plastic ball and tee. If you were giving a persuasive speech about the hazards of smoking, you could use a model or poster of a human head, larynx and chest to graphically illustrate what happens to smokers.

OVERHEAD PROJECTOR

One of the more common visual aids is an overhead projector and pre-prepared transparencies, or power point slides.

> The letters or figures must be large enough for the audience to see easily.

> Only brief, summary points or clear, illustrative diagrams should be put onto each transparency.

One mistake many speakers make is to put practically the whole content of their speech onto transparencies, and then 'read and repeat'.

If members of the audience are hearing and seeing almost exactly the same content, they will lose interest in one or even both sources of the information.

Make sure the transparencies support what you're saying – by summarising only the key words, and illustrating only the key trends.

Your own words can add the colour and background, and thus ensure you keep your listeners with you.

VIDEO

Selected excerpts from a video can also be effective illustrators. Again, the clips should be clearly visible to everyone, pertinent to what you are saying, and short – overlong clips tend to take over a speech and distract the audience from the theme.

If you're going to use any kind of audio-visual aid, here are some tips to make sure they support rather than inhibit your talk.

- Prepare and practise using the aids beforehand.

    NOTE: Few things are more frustrating for a speaker, and an audience, than a visual aid that fails to work.

- Keep your aids simple.

    NOTE: The primary purpose of audio-visual aids is to illustrate what you are saying in more graphic detail.

- Have the aid visible only when you are using it to illustrate a specific point.

- Talk to your audience and not the aid.

    NOTE: It is easy to make the mistake of talking directly to the visual aid while you are showing it rather than to the audience. If you can't turn and directly face the audience, at least stand sideways so you can make reference both to the aid and to your listeners.

EVALUATING AND ASSESSING THE EFFECTIVENESS OF COMMUNICATION

77 Look to Shakespeare!

"Speak the speech, I pray you, as I pronounced it to you - trippingly on the tongue; but if you mouth it, as many of your players do, I has as lief the town crier had spoke my lines. Nor do not saw the air too much with your hand, thus, but use all gently; for in the very torrent, tempest, and as I may say the whirlwind of your passion, you must acquire and beget a temperance that may give it smoothness."

Hamlet act 3 scene 2
William Shakespeare

78 The value of speech criticism

It is important that you develop adequate skills for speech criticism. The ability to evaluate or critique a speech helps you plan and organise your own speeches more effectively and at the same time contributes to greater understanding of oral communication strategies.

In Ancient Greece and Rome, teachers of rhetoric such as Isocrates, Aristotle or Cicero always had their students study classical speeches so they might critique them to learn more about what constituted good rhetorical practices.

As you develop your speech criticism skills, you are developing critical reasoning skills.

79 Evaluating a speech

The three most important areas of speech evaluation are:

> ➢ **organisation**

> ➢ **content**

> ➢ **delivery**

The following speech evaluation questions are solid guidelines – and you should ask yourself these questions as you practise your speech.

NOTE: These guidelines are similar to those developed by the National Communication Association in the United States. They are also the general criteria that you would utilise for evaluating speeches delivered by other people, too.

⇨ **Ask yourself:**

ORGANISATION

Q Was the speech clearly organised?

CONTENT

Q Was the topic appropriate for the audience?

Q Did the topic have depth?

Q Was the topic specific enough?

Q Was the topic limited in scope?

Q Was the topic innovative?

Q Was the speech adapted to suit the audience?

Q Were the main points fully developed?

Q Was speaker credibility established?

Q Were logical and / or emotional appeals effective?

Q Was vivid, descriptive language used?

Q Was the language appropriate?

Q Were any devices used to illustrate and develop ideas?

Q Were visual aids employed and used effectively to help clarify key points?

Q Were the transitions effective?

Q Did the introduction clarify the topic and capture interest?

Q Did the conclusion summarise the main points and leave the audience with a final, specific thought?

Q Were audience questions answered effectively?

DELIVERY

Q Was appropriate dress worn for the occasion?

Q Was posture straight and non-distracting?

Q Were the body movements natural?

Q Was the presentation relaxed in style?

Q Was the style fluent and articulate?

Q Was adequate volume and vocal variety used?

Q Was good visual interaction with the audience maintained?

Q Were expressive and appropriate gestures used?

Q Was there overall control of the topic?

Q Could a desire to communicate with the audience be seen?

The ability to evaluate your own speeches and the speeches given by others is an important part of the process of becoming an effective public communicator.

NOTE: This list of speech evaluation questions should help you in that process but DON'T be limited by it. Add other criteria that you think are beneficial.

The most important step of all is for you to critically evaluate your own speech before you deliver it.

Dos and don'ts:

- DO the best you can with the material you have

- DO make the most of it and enjoy yourself

- DON'T be overly hard on yourself

- DON'T let yourself off the hook

- DON'T allow speech criticism to be personal

Speech evaluation feedback is invaluable and enables the speaker both to experiment and to polish speaking skills.

The purpose of speech criticism should always be recognised as aiming to help the speaker improve his or her speaking ability.

Speech evaluation forms provide us with an easy way to collect data for analysis. Forms such as these are utilized in most basic courses in public speaking in the United States. The two included in Effective Communication are taken from *Public Speaking Handbook: A Liberal Arts Approach,* H Hazel and J Caputo 1998.

Speech evaluation forms can be useful.

Use the SPEECH EVALUATION FORM (see p.196) for an informative or expository speech and the PERSUASIVE SPEECH EVALUATION FORM (see p.197) for a persuasive speech.

80 Evaluating communication - a contextual approach

Having considered the evaluation of the actual performance of a speech, we can now conclude by summarizing the main elements of effective communication in all contexts - with additional consideration of non-native speaker issues which were discussed in PART 1 and PART 3 - MANAGING EFFECTIVE COMMUNICATION IN A VARIETY OF CONTEXTS - Humanistic and cross-cultural considerations.

- A shared knowledge of the purpose of communication, which should be communicated unambiguously

- A shared understanding of what is already known

- The relationship between the communicators and the L1s of the communicators

- The type of communication i.e. one-way as in a lecture, two-way as in a conversation, multi-way as in a seminar

- A shared knowledge of the conventions of communication with reference to the relationship between the communicators and the type of communication

- A logical, progressive communication process appropriate for the communicative dynamic

- Clarity and appropriateness of speech i.e. use of grammar and vocabulary, degree of formality of language used, phonological competence of communicators

- A degree of aural understanding, which will be dependent on each of the above-mentioned elements as well as on the listening skills of the communicators

- Mutual understanding in summary and conclusion

If the teachers, students and aficionados of Effective Communication consider these elements as the basis of preparation, process and evaluation in every communicative context, the objectives of developing the skills essential to purposeful communication, and the constructive reflection on the success of the communicative event, will be achieved.

SPEECH EVALUATION FORM

Speaker_____

Evaluator_____

Grade_____

SUPERIOR	VERY GOOD	GOOD	NEEDS MUCH WORK	Organization	Comments
				Introduction	
				Gets attention	
				Rapport with audience	
				States purpose/central idea	
				Transitions to Body	
				Body	
				Main points clear/organized	
				Outline format	
				Content	
				Development of key points	
				Conclusion	
				Summary/Review	
				Compelling Final Statement	
				Delivery	
				Verbal	
				Projection	
				Voice rate	
				Voice pitch/variety	
				Articulation	
				Quality	
				Nonverbal	
				Appearance: outfit appropriate to the occasion	
				Eye contact	
				Gestures	
				Body Language	
				Smile/Facial expression	
				Visual Aids	
				Blended with speech	
				Handling during talk	

Summary Comments:

PERSUASIVE SPEECH EVALUATION FORM

Speaker_____

Evaluator_____

Grade_____

What did you especially like?_____
_____

In your opinion, how could the speech be improved? _____
_____

SUPERIOR	VERY GOOD	GOOD	NEEDS MUCH WORK	PLEASE COMMENT ON ANY OF THE FOLLOWING AREAS (BE SPECIFIC)	COMMENTS
				Did the speaker formulate an effective persuasive strategy?	
				Did the speaker establish ethos?	
				Did the speaker analyze and adapt to audience?	
				Were arguments supported with enough evidence?	
				Were emotional appeals effective?	
				Did the speaker appear to have a clear persuasive purpose?	
				Did the speaker establish "common ground" with the audience?	

Summary Comments:

DRAMATIC LINES HANDBOOKS in association with
Trinity, The International Examinations Board

EFFECTIVE COMMUNICATION
ISBN 1 904557 13 9

John Caputo, Jo Palosaari and Ken Pickering

☐

ACTING SHAKESPEARE FOR AUDITIONS AND EXAMINATIONS
ISBN 1 904557 10 4

Frank Barrie

☐

SPEECH AND DRAMA
ISBN 1 904557 15 5

Ann Jones and Robert Cheeseman

☐

THINKING ABOUT PLAYS
ISBN 1 904557 14 7

Ken Pickering Giles and Auckland-Lewis

☐

PREPARING FOR YOUR DIPLOMA IN DRAMA AND SPEECH
ISBN 1 904557 11 2

Kirsty N Findlay and Ken Pickering

☐

MUSICAL THEATRE
ISBN 1 904557 12 0

Gerry Tebbutt

ADDITIONAL TITLES AVAILABLE

All books may be ordered direct from:

DRAMATIC LINES PO BOX 201 TWICKENHAM TW2 5RQ ENGLAND

freefone: 0800 5429570
t: 020 8296 9503
f: 020 8296 9503
e: mail@dramaticlinespublishers.co.uk
www.dramaticlines.co.uk

MONOLOGUES

THE SIEVE   Heather Stephens
AND OTHER SCENES   ISBN 0 9522224 0 X

The Sieve contains unusual short original monologues valid for junior acting examinations. The material in The Sieve has proved popular with winning entries worldwide in drama festival competitions. Although these monologues were originally written for the 8-14 year age range they have been used by adult actors for audition and performance pieces. Each monologue is seen through the eyes of a young person with varied subject matter including tough social issues such as fear, 'Television Spinechiller', senile dementia , 'Seen Through a Glass Darkly' and withdrawal from the world in 'The Sieve'. Other pieces include: 'A Game of Chicken', 'The Present', 'Balloon Race' and a widely used new adaptation of Hans Christian Andersen's 'The Little Match Girl' in monologue form.

CABBAGE   Heather Stephens
AND OTHER SCENES   ISBN 0 9522224 5 0

Following the success of The Sieve, Heather Stephens has written an additional book of monologues with thought provoking and layered subject matter valid for junior acting examinations. The Cabbage monologues were originally written for the 8-14 year age range but have been used by adult actors for audition and performance pieces. The Aberfan slag-heap disaster issues are graphically confronted in 'Aberfan Prophecy' and 'The Surviving Twin' whilst humorous perceptions of life are observed by young people in 'The Tap Dancer' and 'Cabbage'. Other pieces include: 'The Dinner Party Guest', 'Nine Lives' and a new adaptation of Robert Browning's 'The Pied Piper' seen through the eyes of the crippled child.

ALONE IN MY ROOM
ORIGINAL MONOLOGUES

Ken Pickering
ISBN 0 9537770 0 6

This collection of short original monologues includes extracts from the author's longer works in addition to the classics. Provocative issues such as poverty and land abuse are explored in 'One Child at a Time', 'The Young Person Talks' and 'Turtle Island' with adaptations from 'Jane Eyre', Gulliver's Travels' and 'Oliver Twist' and well loved authors include Dostoyevsky. These monologues have a wide variety of applications including syllabus recommendation for various acting examinations. Each monologue has a brief background description and acting notes.

DUOLOGUES

PEARS

Heather Stephens
ISBN 0 9522224 6 9

These thought provoking and unusual short original duologues provide new material for speech and drama festival candidates in the 8-14 year age range. The scenes have also been widely used for junior acting examinations and in a variety of school situations and theatrical applications. Challenging topics in Pears include the emotive issues of child migration, 'Blondie', 'The Outback Institution' and bullying 'Bullies', other scenes examine friendship, 'The Best of Friends', 'The Row' and envy, 'Never the Bridesmaid'. New adaptations of part scenes from 'Peace' by Aristophanes and 'Oliver Twist' by Charles Dickens are also included.

TOGETHER NOW
ORIGINAL DUOLOGUES

Ken Pickering
ISBN 0 9537770 1 4

This collection of short duologues includes extracts from Ken Pickering's longer works together with new original pieces. The variety of experiences explored in the scenes can all be easily identified with, such as an awkward situation, 'You Tell Her', and the journey of self-knowledge in 'Gilgamesh', whilst 'Mobile phones', 'Sales' and 'Food' observe realistic situations in an interesting and perceptive way. Other duologues based on well-known stories include 'Snow White' and 'The Pilgrim's Progress'. Each piece has a brief background description and acting notes. The scenes have syllabus recommendation for a number of examination boards and wide variety of theatrical and school applications.

MONOLOGUES AND DUOLOGUES
SHAKESPEARE THE REWRITES   Claire Jones
ISBN 0 9522224 8 5

A collection of short monologues and duologues for female players. The scenes are from rewrites of Shakespeare plays from 1670 to the present day written by authors seeking to embellish original texts for performances, to add prequels or sequels or satisfy their own very personal ideas about production. This material is fresh and unusual and will provide exciting new audition and examination material. Comparisons with the original Shakespeare text are fascinating and this book will provide a useful contribution to Theatre Study work from GCSE to beyond 'A' level. Contributors include James Thurber (Macbeth) Arnold Wesker (Merchant of Venice) and Peter Ustinov (Romanoff and Juliet). The collection also includes a most unusual Japanese version of Hamlet.

RESOURCES
DRAMA LESSONS IN ACTION   Antoinette Line
ISBN 0 9522224 2 6

Resource material suitable for classroom and assembly use for teachers of junior and secondary age pupils. Lessons are taught through improvisation, these are not presented as 'model lessons' but provide ideas for adaptation and further development. Lessons include warm-up and speech exercises and many themes are developed through feelings such as timidity, resentfulness, sensitivity and suspicion. Material can be used by groups of varying sizes and pupils are asked to respond to texts from a diverse selection of well known authors including: Roald Dahl, Ogden Nash, John Betjeman, Ted Hughes, Michael Rosen, and Oscar Wilde.

AAARGH TO ZIZZ   Graeme Talboys
135 DRAMA GAMES   ISBN 0 9537770 5 7

This valuable resource material has been created by a drama teacher and used mostly in formal drama lessons but also in informal situations such as clubs and parties. The games are extremely flexible, from warm up to cool down, inspiration to conclusion and from deadly serious to purest fun and the wide variety ranges from laughing and rhythm activities to building a sentence and word association. Many games could be used as part of a PSHE programme together with activities connected with 'fair play'. The games are easily adapted and each has notes on setting up details of straightforward resources needed. All this material has been used with a wide range of young people in the 10 - 18 year age range.

DRAMA·DANCE·SINGING edited by John Nicholas
TEACHER RESOURCE BOOK   ISBN 0 9537770 2 2

This collection of drama, dance and singing lesson activities has been drawn from a bank of ideas used by the Stagecoach Theatre Arts Schools teachers. Clearly presented lessons include speech and drama exercises, games and improvisations often developed as a response to emotions. Dance activities include warm-ups, basic dance positions, improvisations, versatile dance exercises and routines, while singing activities help to develop rhythm and notation as well as providing enjoyable games to develop the voice. Activities can be easily adapted for large or small group use and are suitable for 6 - 16 year olds in a fun yet challenging way.

MUSICAL PLAYS

THREE CHEERS FOR MRS BUTLER   adapted by Vicky Ireland
ISBN 0 9537770 4 9

This versatile musical play about everyday school life is for anyone who has ever been to school. It features the poems and characters created by Allan Ahlberg with a foreword by Michael Rosen, songs by Colin Matthews and Steven Markwick and was first performed at the Polka Theatre for Children, London. The two acts of 40 minutes each can be performed by children, adults or a mixture of both and the play can be produced with a minimum cast of 7 or a large cast of any size, with or without music and songs, as well as having a wide variety of other musical and dramatic applications.

INTRODUCING OSCAR   Veronica Bennetts
The Selfish Giant & The Happy Prince   ISBN 0 9537770 3 0

Oscar Wilde's timeless stories for children have been chosen for adaptation because of the rich opportunities offered for imaginative exploration and the capacity to vividly illuminate many aspects of the human condition. The original dialogue, lyrics and music by Veronica Bennetts can be adapted and modified according to the needs of pupils, individual schools or drama groups. The Selfish Giant runs for 25 minutes and The Happy Prince for 1 hour 15 minutes. Both musical can be used for Trinity College, *London.* examinations and are ideal for end of term productions, for drama groups and primary and secondary schools.

A CD backing track for The Selfish Giant & The Happy Prince is available.

TEENAGE PLAYS

WHAT IS THE MATTER WITH MARY JANE?   Wendy Harmer
ISBN 0 9522224 4 2

This monodrama about a recovering anorexic and bulimic takes the audience into the painful reality of a young woman afflicted by eating disorders. The play is based on the personal experience of actress Sancia Robinson and has proved hugely popular in Australia. It is written with warmth and extraordinary honesty and the language, humour and style appeal to current youth culture. A study guide for teachers and students is included in this English edition ensuring that the material is ideal for use in the secondary school classroom and for PSHE studies, drama departments in schools and colleges in addition to amateur and professional performance.

X-STACY   Margery Forde
ISBN 0 9522224 9 3

Margery Forde's powerful play centres on the rave culture and illicit teenage drug use and asks tough questions about family, friends and mutual responsibilities. The play has proved hugely successful in Australia and this English edition is published with extensive teachers' notes by Helen Radian, Lecturer of Drama at Queensland University of Technology, to enrich its value for the secondary school classroom, PSHE studies, English and drama departments.

ASSEMBLIES

ASSEMBLIES! ASSEMBLIES! ASSEMBLIES!   Kryssy Hurley
ISBN 0 9537770 6 5

These teacher-led assemblies require minimum preparation and have been written by a practising teacher to involve small or large groups. Each assembly lasts 15-20 minutes and is suitable for Key Stages 2 and 3. There are 12 for each term and these explore many PSHE and Citizenship issues including bullying, racism, friendship, co-operation, feeling positive, making responsible choices and decisions, school rules and laws outside school. All have the following sections: *Resource and Organisation, What To Do, Reflection Time and Additional Resources and Activities.* The assemblies are both enjoyable and informative for pupils participating and audiences alike.

SCENES FOR TWO TO TEN PLAYERS

JELLY BEANS — Joseph McNair Stover
ISBN 0 9522224 7 7

The distinctive style and deceptively simple logic of American writer Joseph McNair Stover has universal appeal with scenes that vary in tone from whimsical to serious and focus on young peoples relationships in the contemporary world. The 10 to 15 minute original scenes for 2, 3, and 4 players are suitable for 11 year old students through to adult. Minimal use of sets and props makes Jelly Beans ideal for group acting examinations, classroom drama, assemblies, and a wide variety of additional theatrical applications.

SCENES 4 3 2 10 PLAYERS — Sandy Hill
ISBN 0 9537770 8 1

There are 10 original scenes in the book written for 3 to 10 players with opportunities for doubling-up of characters and introduction of optional additional players. The versatile scenes are of varying playing times and are suitable for performers from as young as 7 through to adult. The flexible use of sets and props have made these pieces particularly useful for group acting examinations and have proved to be immediately popular and successful for candidates as well as winning entries at drama festivals, they can also be used effectively for classroom drama and school assemblies. The scenes are often quirky and vary in tone with unusual endings. They will be enjoyed by performers and audiences alike.

ONE ACT PLAYS

WILL SHAKESPEARE SAVE US! — Paul Nimmo
WILL SHAKESPEARE SAVE THE KING!   ISBN 0 9522224 1 8

Two versatile plays in which famous speeches and scenes from Shakespeare are acted out as part of a comic story about a bored king and his troupe of players. These plays are suitable for the 11-18 year age range and have been produced with varying ages within the same cast and also performed by adults to a young audience. The plays can be produced as a double bill, alternatively each will stand on its own, performed by a minimum cast of 10 without a set, few props and modern dress or large cast, traditional set and costumes. The scripts are ideal for reading aloud by classes or groups and provide an excellent introduction to the works of Shakespeare. Both plays have been successfully performed on tour and at the Shakespeare's Globe in London.

SUGAR ON SUNDAYS
AND OTHER PLAYS

Andrew Gordon
ISBN 0 9522224 3 4

A collection of six one act plays bringing history alive through drama. History is viewed through the eyes of ordinary people and each play is packed with details about everyday life, important events and developments of the period. The plays can be used as classroom drama, for school performances and group acting examinations and also as shared texts for the literacy hour. The plays are suitable for children from Key Stage 2 upwards and are 40-50 minutes in length and explore Ancient Egypt, Ancient Greece, Anglo-Saxon and Viking Times, Victorian Britain and the Second World War. A glossary of key words helps to develop children's historical understanding of National Curriculum History Topics and the plays provide opportunities for children to enjoy role-play and performance.